SOFT FURNISHING

Kitty Ward, although interested in needlework from an early age, did not start to study it seriously until 1966 when she enrolled for the City and Guilds Dress course, passing the Advanced stage in 1969. She went on to take the City and Guilds Soft Furnishing and Upholstery course rather as a 'second' subject for the Teaching Certificate, sitting the Advanced exam in 1972 when she passed with Distinction. Gradually, however, she found that Soft Furnishing played a greater part than Dress in her career.

Mrs Ward has been a member of the Embroiderers Guild since 1966, attending many of their courses, including Lace Making, and she attended the Harrow College of Technology to take the City and Guilds Embroidery Certificate.

Since 1970, Mrs Ward has been teaching Further Education classes in a number of subjects including Embroidery, Lace Making, Pattern Cutting, Dressmaking and, of course, Soft Furnishing and Upholstery (including the City and Guilds course).

Early in 1973 Mrs Ward started, through NADFAS, to go to Woburn Abbey one day a week to help keep it 'stately'. From this, her interest in the care of old textiles has grown, and she is a member of the Group for Costume and Textile staff in Museums. She now divides her time between part-time teaching at Cassio College, Watford, and caring for the textiles at Woburn Abbey where she has a work room and her work involves all kinds of repair, renovation and conservation. She has recently been accepted as a member of the Association of Master Upholsterers.

TEACH YOURSELF BOOKS

SOFT FURNISHING

Kitty Ward

TEACH YOURSELF BOOKS
Hodder and Stoughton

Contents

Introduction

Learning to make soft furnishings, like all similar crafts, involves acquiring a series of basic skills which can then be combined together in various ways to produce a variety of different articles.

This book is set out in two parts: the first part describes essential soft furnishing skills, starting from those probably already familiar to many through everyday repairs and household needlework, and progressing to the less familiar and more specialised. The second part describes how to make simple examples of the main soft furnishing articles.

By approaching the subject like this, it is hoped that, depending on your ability and background knowledge, you will be able to use the book in one of three ways: to start from the beginning and work through the skills to the articles; to select the articles you want to make and check back to any skill you are uncertain of; or to use the book simply for reference when a particular problem arises.

Both metric and imperial measurements are used. However the equivalents are approximate and do not correlate, so articles may not make up to exactly the same size in either measurement. Therefore you should follow either metric or imperial throughout the making of a particular article.

Abbreviation
Please note that throughout, WS represents Wrong Side and RS represents Right Side.

PART 1

1   Making the right start

Many people are discouraged from embarking on making articles for the home because, unlike dressmaking, it is not usually possible to go out and buy a paper pattern with instructions on fabric requirements, cutting, making up etc. One of the main purposes of this book is to give you the background and confidence to take up soft furnishing. This chapter covers the basic equipment you will need and gives some tips on important, but often neglected points.

Seam allowance

To ensure the correct size and fit in soft furnishings it is necessary to work to an *accurate seam allowance*. In dressmaking emphasis is placed on the fitting line which is carefully marked; in soft furnishing, provided an accurate seam allowance is followed throughout the cutting and making-up stages, marking is usually unnecessary.

The width of the seam allowance will depend on the type of fabric being used. On firmly woven fabric, it can be as little as 13 mm ($\frac{1}{2}$ in), but many furnishing fabrics are loosely woven and need a larger allowance. A good guide is to look at the actual threads making up the weave and ensure that *at least* four threads are taken into the seam allowance – preferably more.

Handling methods during making up

Soft furnishing articles have to stand hard wear, but of a different kind from dressmaking. Less emphasis needs to be placed on inside finishes which are not frequently handled, nor are fastenings likely to be undone more than once a year. Hand-stitching can often be larger and looser with more emphasis placed on the part that is seen. On the other hand, heavier fabrics are often used, seams have to be very firm indeed, and a stronger thread is frequently needed matched to the life expectancy of the article, especially on the parts that have greatest wear.

It is often necessary to handle large expanses of material at a time, and it is worth cultivating an 'organised' approach when making soft furnishings. Here are some suggestions:

1.   Cutting out

(*a*) Mark the lines to be cut carefully with chalk before cutting into the fabric and *check* the measurements before starting.

(*b*) When cutting several pieces for, say, a loose cover, label each piece with chalk as you cut it, keeping the label to the *top* of the piece, thus ensuring that it cannot be set the wrong way up during assembly.

(*c*) If the pieces are large, fold them neatly so that the label shows.

(*d*) Many fabrics fray badly and, if working with a minimum seam allowance, overcast the raw edges immediately. This can be done by hand, or by sewing machine using a stepped zig-zag (*see* Chapter 3). If your machine only does the simple zig-zag, it is wiser to hand-overcast (*see* Chapter 3) as the ordinary zig-zag tends to pull more threads off the edge.

2.   Making-up aids

It is worthwhile getting used to using two soft furnishing aids – the template (Fig. 1) and the weight.

The template is a piece of card on which you notch all turning allowances needed for a particular article. If, for example, you are making a lined curtain with a side hem of 4 cm (1½ in) and a double hem of 5 cm (2 in) your template would look like Fig. 1.

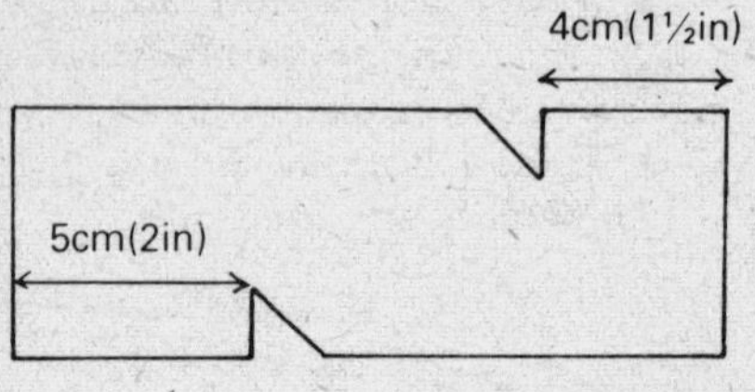

Figure 1   *A template*

Provided that your fabric can be ironed, it can be taken straight to the ironing board after cutting out (and joining) to press (*a*) the seams, (*b*) a 4 cm (1½ in) side hem each side, running the template down as you iron, and (*c*) a double hem at the bottom, turning up 5 cm (2 in) at a time. From this stage it is a simple matter of pressing in the correct mitres (*see* Chapter 10) and inserting a few pins ready for stitching.

The *weight* is a heavy object such as a brick, old iron, or whatever, covered in fabric to which you can pin the right-hand edge (if you are right-handed) of the article on which you are hand-stitching. This enables you to pull against the weight lightly with the left hand, holding the hem, or edge, in place for stitching with the right hand. This not only speeds up the sewing process but also maintains an even tension and avoids the tendency for the top layer of fabric to ease over the lower when worked in the hand.

It is often possible to move straight from the 'ironing board' stage to the 'weight' stage with the minimum of pinning and no tacking.

3.   Basic tools and equipment

Most households have the usual needlework equipment needed for soft furnishings. The following list covers everything you are likely to need.

Sewing machine

It does not matter if you only have an old machine. The basic requirement is that it should stitch evenly and have a presser-foot attachment enabling it to stitch close to the piping. A simple zig-zag is useful, and special bonuses are a stepped (or waved) zig-zag and a cording foot. It is an advantage, too, if the machine can be foot-operated, as both hands are generally needed to control fabric bulk.

If planning to buy a new machine with soft furnishings in mind, choose a robust one which has provision for the presser-foot to ride over a wide range of thicknesses of fabric. A firm flat working surface is needed, and a machine with plenty of space under the body, to the right of the presser-foot, as this is useful when tackling something bulky where much of it is lying under the machine. As a general rule, robustness is of more importance than a range of decorative stitches.

Measure

A 3 metre (9 ft) steel rule is of more use than a tape measure. Not only do you need the extra length, but a rigid rule is more accurate for taking measurements of windows, beds etc.

Scissors

The essential here is that they should be sharp *right up to the points*. Making soft furnishings involves a lot of snipping into notches, corners etc., which is difficult if the points of the scissors are blunt.

Pins

For general use ordinary dressmakers steel pins are suitable, but, if you can possibly get hold of a few long soft white brass pins, these are the safest to use when fitting loose covers as there is a risk of the steel pins snapping in the upholstery. These long soft pins are also invaluable when working on loose-weave fabrics. Antimacassar pins (which can sometimes be bought on a card) are useful for holding fabric in place on furniture.

Needles
Besides the ordinary range of sewing needles, useful additions are:
(*a*) Leather needles (both for hand and machine) which are useful not only for leather but also for coated fabrics like vinyl and PVC. They have bayonet points which cut smoothly through stiff and heavy fabrics.
(*b*) Semi-circular upholstery needle. This can often be obtained on a card in a set of 'household' or 'craft' needles and the most useful size is a fairly fine one with a diameter of about 4 cm (1½ in). It is marvellous for stitching in awkward places where there is no room to pull a straight needle through. It takes a little practice to use, but rewards the effort.
(*c*) A heavy needle for stitching thick fabrics with an eye large enough to thread with strong heavy thread.
(*d*) A buttoning (or mattress) needle. This is a very long needle (a 20 cm (8 in) one is a useful length) with a point each end. Handle it with respect and keep the points protected with corks or tucked into a strip of foam. This is essential for putting central buttons into cushions and useful for replacing buttons on mattresses etc.

Thimble
Essential, as so often one has to force the needle through many thicknesses of heavy fabric.

Threads
Heavy threads have already been mentioned and you should try to build up a stock of these. They can be purchased as button thread. Some manufacturers sell a heavy quality thread for buttonholes, and it can be picked up sometimes in stock clearance sales of shoe-makers, boating and camping gear specialists – even in shops selling fishing equipment. Also some of the finer threads sold for crochet (e.g. Coats Chain Mercer) are useful for hand-gathering and stitching on curtain hooks etc.
   Buy a big spool of white tacking thread as, with such long stretches to be tacked, it is wasteful to use good sewing thread.

Tailor's chalk
You will need white and one other colour.

Working space
This is probably the hardest thing to provide, but is vital as large articles

need to be spread out at times during the making-up process. If you haven't a large table, it is worth buying a piece of hardboard (or two pieces hinged together) at least 122 cm (48 in) wide and as long as possible, which can be placed over your dining-table. Ensure that the corners are square as these can be used when cutting curtains. The only alternative is working on the floor which can be tiring. It is worth bearing in mind that it is pointless to attempt the making of an article larger than your available workspace.

2   Choosing your fabric

There is a large amount of literature available on every aspect of fabrics
and fibres. This chapter considers them only as they affect soft furnishings,
but for more general information consult the titles included in the further
reading list.

Many people wonder why some fabrics are sold for furnishings and some
for dress, and if they are really interchangeable. These days fabrics can be
produced for specific end-uses through variations in the fibre used, and the
construction, dyeing and finishing processes. The requirements of fabric
for furnishings differ from those of dressmaking and can be summed up as
the need for durability versus the need for wearability. Fabric for wearing
must be supple and comfortable, able to stand a lot of handling and movement in wear, be patterned in proportion to its wearer, not be too heavy
and possibly stand frequent washing but not constant exposure to light.
On the other hand, furnishing fabric does not need to be supple or light
but may need a good drape, have colour and a pattern suited to the proportions of a room, rather than a person, need not be washable or tolerate a lot
of movement, but must be resistant to fading, abrasion and attack by moth
and mildew. Soft furnishing fabrics can be made with more emphasis on
interesting textures and weaves that would be unsuitable for clothing.

One of the most obvious differences has always been in the width in
which fabrics for furnishings are sold, usually 122 cm (48 in). This proves
very convenient when estimating quantities, particularly where fabrics and
linings must match.

Fabric construction most common in soft furnishing fabrics

The majority of furnishing fabrics are *woven*, i.e. *warp* threads running the
length of the cloth are interwoven with *weft* threads running across the
fabric from one edge to the other where they are generally woven more
firmly, or stronger threads are introduced, to form the selvedge. The
strongest way of the fabric is always in the *warp* direction – *never* be
tempted to hang curtains etc. with the weft threads vertical, except in the
case of the specially constructed net ones, of course.

The most common *knitted* fabric used for furnishings is that made for stretch covers, but this is seldom obtainable retail.

Another knitted fabric which frequently appears in the stores is actually composed to two knitted fabrics *bonded* together and sold as 'ready-lined' curtaining or 'bonded nylon velvet'. Because of the bond it is dimensionally stable but has a rather stiff drape.

Co-we-knit and stitch-bonding are cheaper methods of production than weaving in which a web of fibre is consolidated into a fabric by being fed into a type of warp-knitting machine called a Mali which forms lines of nearly invisible chain-stitch. The resultant stable, non-fray, easy-care fabric is sold widely for curtaining under trade names such as 'Astrocord' and 'Duracord'.

A fabric called Cambrelle, developed by ICI is coming into the furnishings range; this is made of a special bicomponent nylon fibre which during manufacture of the cloth is subjected to heat which causes one of the components to melt, compacting the cloth so that it becomes dense and stable. At present it results in a rather rigid cloth but is recommended for loose covers because not only is it hard-wearing but, due to its lack of permeability, it prevents dust from penetrating.

Coated fabrics are occasionally used for cushion covers etc. They are composed of a knitted or woven cloth coated in vinyl or urethane and although hard-wearing are not easy to handle because they are bulky and rigid, and their rather sticky surface will not travel smoothly under the machine foot.

Non-wovens include leather, felt, and a range of synthetic fabrics sold mainly for interlinings, e.g. Vilene, useful for stiffening curtain headings and pelmets.

Choosing fabrics for specific items

Cushions
Almost any fabric is suitable for a cushion, dependent on its purpose, but you should consider:

1. Whether it will need to be washed.
2. What use it will have and whether it will get crushed and creased.

Curtains
Here the choice is more complicated (*see* Chapter 13). Bearing in mind the function of the curtains and the colour scheme, additional points to consider are:

1. Whether the fabric is colour-fast.

2.   The drape, particularly in relation to the *length* of the curtain, i.e. don't choose too bulky a fabric for a short window.
3.   Similarly, size of pattern should be to the scale of the window.
4.   Fabric for unlined curtains should be reversible.
5.   If the fabric is intended for washable curtains, check shrink-resistance.

Loose covers
For these, the fabric must:

1.   be dense enough to prevent dust penetrating;
2.   not crease excessively;
3.   withstand abrasion and hard wear;
4.   be washable.

Note: After washing covers it is recommended that they are put back on the chairs damp and ironed in situ – this helps to resist shrinkage.

Bedcovers
Bedcovers usually receive minimal wear and tear except for daily folding, so the choice of fabric is wide. Points to bear in mind are:

1.   Whether the fabric needs to be washable.
2.   The ability of the fabric to hold pleats if you are planning a pleated valance – some of the easy-care fabrics will not do this.

Fabrics that need special care in handling

Dupion
This is a very popular fabric with its 'wild silk' appearance and wide range of available colours. However, because it is now made mostly from synthetic lustrous fibres it is of very unstable construction and frays badly. Two rules have to be observed:

1.   Allow for generous seams and turnings.
2.   Do not cut the fabric until you are ready *immediately* to overcast all cut edges.

Loosely woven acrylics
A wide range of these are sold, mainly for semi-sheer curtains. They do not seam up into shapes well, the weave being too widely spaced for narrow turnings and too bulky for wide ones. Unless the selvedge is spoiling the hang of a curtain, it is best left to form the curtain edge. If for any reason the selvedge has to be cut off, the alternative is either a double hem, or possibly the fraying back of the edge to a line of zig-zag or hem-stitching to form a fringe.

Velvet
Most modern furnishing velvets have the pile laid in one direction which can be felt by running the hand up and down in the direction of the warp. Furnishings are usually made up with the pile lying downwards to avoid trapping dust, and care must be taken to cut and make up each piece in the same direction.

Machining seams can be a problem as one pile face tends to ride over the other. Careful tacking and machining can usually cope with this problem but it sometimes helps if pins, set at right angles to the seam, are left in for the machine to ride over. Other ways of making stitching easier are:

1.   Reducing the pressure on the presser-foot slightly.
2.   Placing tissue between the pile faces, machining through it, and pulling it away after the seam has been stitched.

If you haven't access to a velvet board (a board covered in tiny wire prongs upon which the velvet is placed, face down, and pressed on the WS) the best way to press long seams is to enlist the aid of someone to hold one end whilst you hold the other taut and press gently along it.

Piping can present problems in velvet and it is worth considering applying cord instead.

Bonded fabrics
Machining these can have similar problems to velvet because the foot is apt to 'bed' into the double fabric. Try the methods of making stitching easier given above.

Coated fabrics, leathercloth, leather
If you *must* use any of these, follow these rules:

1.   Use a longer machine stitch than usual and never go over the same line of machining twice.
2.   Make sure your stitching is right first time – unpicking will leave a line of holes.
3.   If the fabric sticks under the presser-foot try:
(*a*) easing the pressure on the presser-foot;
(*b*) dusting the surface with talcum powder or chalk;
(*c*) using a *roller foot* on the machine (obtainable for most makes) which has a textured roller that wheels along;
(*d*) buying a special leather needle.

Using patterned fabric
Patterned fabric plays such an important part in soft furnishings that a few points are worth mentioning:

1.   On any article the pattern needs to be centred, placed right way up, and matched across or lined up on each important section of the article.
2.   Patterns with parallel and horizontal stripes need to be aligned with the floor, walls and ceiling rather than the furniture.
3.   When deciding which way up to set a flower spray, bear in mind the way the plant naturally grows. Fortunately, nowadays, manufacturers obligingly put a directional arrow in the fabric margin, as whole classes have been known to fall out on this subject, but if it isn't obvious it doesn't matter!
4.   When choosing a pattern, try to see it from a distance as it is possible that a small insignificant spray will develop into a repeating stripe that needs to be matched.
5.   Beware, especially at sale times, of patterns that have been printed very much 'off the grain'. Patterns usually repeat at least once across a fabric width: check that the second repeat follows fairly closely along the warp thread. If it is more than, say 2·5 cm (1 in) out, all kinds of problems arise, particularly in curtains where the sides should be at right angles to the hem and yet the pattern must be level along the hem.
6.   *Pattern matching*
Bear in mind the following points when buying and handling patterned material:

(*a*) The majority of patterned fabrics match across the horizontal line, but sometimes the match drops down diagonally half a pattern (called the half-drop in the trade).
(*b*) If buying hand-blocked fabric do not rely on a near-invisible match, selvedge to selvedge, when joining widths. Very often not only does the width of the selvedge margin alter but the pattern definition is irregular and inaccurate also.
(*c*) When patterned fabric appears to be wider than the usual 122 cm (48 in) do not assume that the final joined width will be more too, as often much of the extra width is taken up by a very wide unpatterned margin filled with writing and spare pattern beyond the matching point.

3 Stitches and seam finishes

1. Tacking – basting (Fig. 2)
Three types of tacking are used in soft furnishing:

(*a*) Straight tacking taking alternate long and short stitches (Fig. 2a).
(*b*) Diagonal tacking, which holds two layers or more of fabric together and prevents slippage (Fig. 2b).
(*c*) Slip-tacking, useful for pattern matching and positioning seams (Fig. 2c).

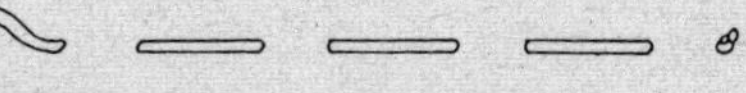

Figure 2a   Straight tacking

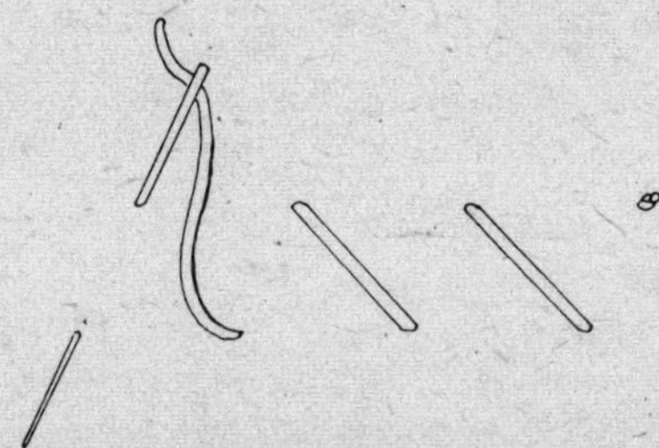

Figure 2b   Diagonal tacking

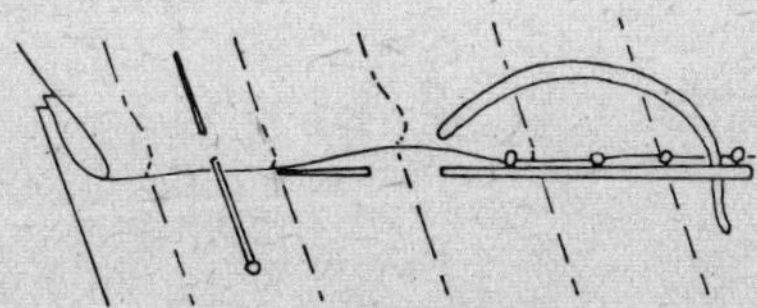

Figure 2c   Slip tacking

Method: Work from RS. Pin seam in lapped position, i.e. one piece turned under and lapped over the other piece where the seam is to be. Run the needle 6–12 mm ($\frac{1}{4}$ in–$\frac{1}{2}$ in) along the folded edge and exactly opposite where the thread emerges insert the needle into the underlying fabric along the seam line. This will given an even line of tacking stitches on the WS.

2. Half back stitch   (Fig. 3)

This is used when a firm hand-stitch is needed that shows as a near-invisible stitch on the right side with a rather longer stitch on the wrong side. The appearance of the stitch on the back will vary in length depending on the thickness of the number of the layers of fabric. Worked from the RS.

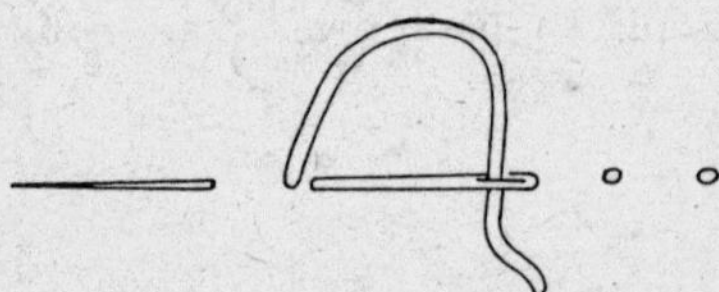

Figure 3   Half back stitch

3. Stab-stitch   (Fig. 4)

This looks like a small running stitch but each stitch is worked individually, stabbing first down and then up. Stab-stitch is used when the thickness of work prevents using small running stitch.

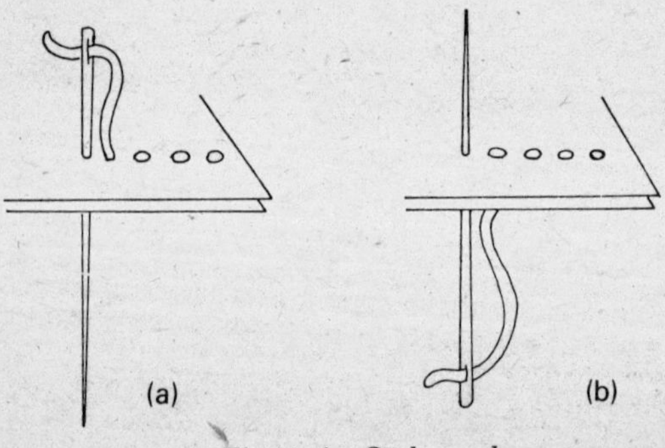

Figure 4   Stab-stitch

4. Slip-stitch (ladder-stitch) (Fig. 5)

This is used to draw two edges together invisibly so that they look like a machined seam. The needle is run first along one folded edge, then the other, always inserting the point directly opposite where the thread emerged. (This stitch is used a great deal in upholstery and worked with a semi-circular needle.)

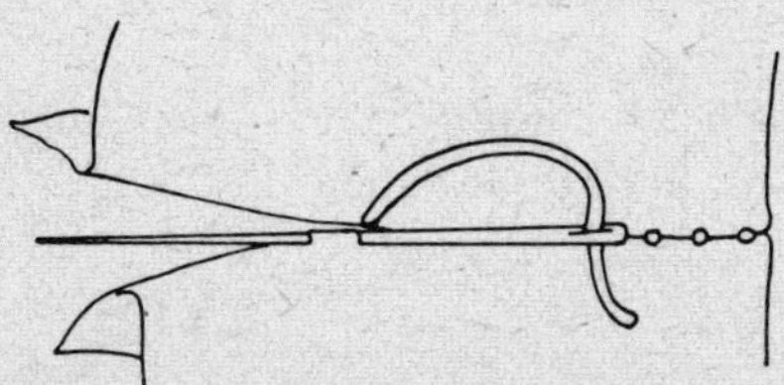

Figure 5   Slip-stitch

5. Slip-hemming (Fig. 6)

As in dressmaking, this is used to turn up hems. The point of the needle is run along the hem edge, emerging to pick up a tiny stitch on the underlying fabric. In soft furnishing the stitch running along the hem edge can be about 13 mm ($\frac{1}{2}$ in) long and is never pulled tight as this produces a hem ridge.

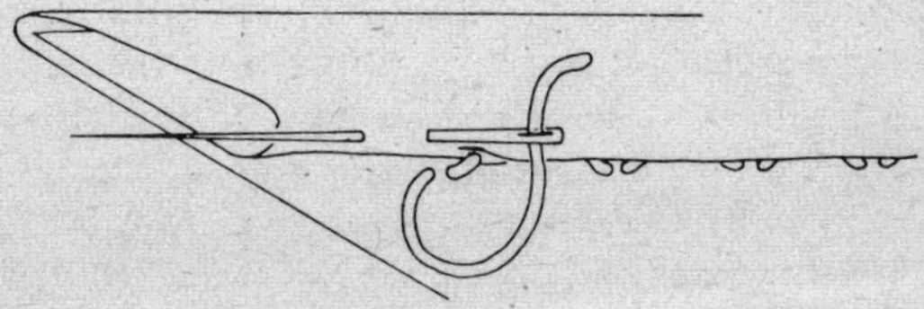

Figure 6   Slip-hemming

6. Overcasting (Fig. 7)

This is used to neaten raw edges and prevent fraying. (Worked from left to right.)

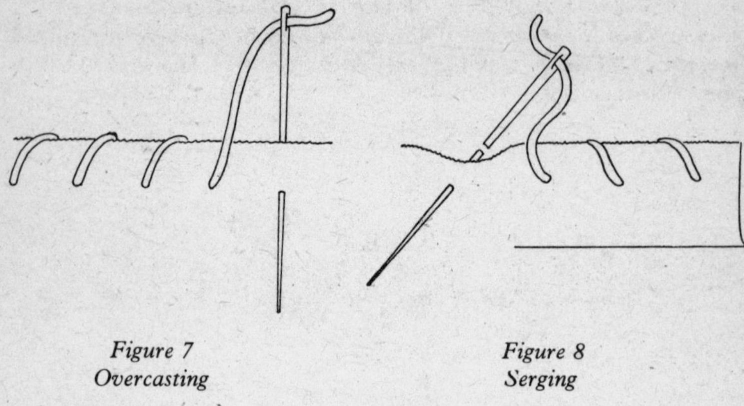

Figure 7
Overcasting

Figure 8
Serging

7. Serging (Fig. 8)

This combines overcasting with hemming and is worked over the raw edge from right to left. One or two threads of the face fabric are picked up whilst the needle goes deeply into the raw edge of 6–13 mm ($\frac{1}{4}$ in–$\frac{1}{2}$ in) depending on the fray of the fabric.

8. Locking (Fig. 9)

This is a special stitch used for holding two layers of fabric loosely together, e.g. curtain fabric to lining, so that they do not float apart. It should not be visible from the front or back of the article, nor should it be a rigid hold. It is worked like an elongated 'blanket stitch' down the length of the article picking up a thread from the face fabric and lining on the needle and leaving a space between stitches of 10–15 cm (4 in–6 in). Try to complete a line of locking on one thread, but if this is impracticable, knot a new length to the old about halfway between stitches so that the thread remains mobile. *Do not pull the thread tight*, but keep looped tension by inserting your hand in the trailing thread between stitches.

9. Buttonhole Bar (Fig. 10)

This is used to reinforce seam ends subject to strain and as an alternative to metal bars for hooks. Use strong thread and, after taking two or three stitches across, work buttonhole stitch into the 'bar' thus formed. Work with the needle reversed to avoid catching fabric in with the bar.

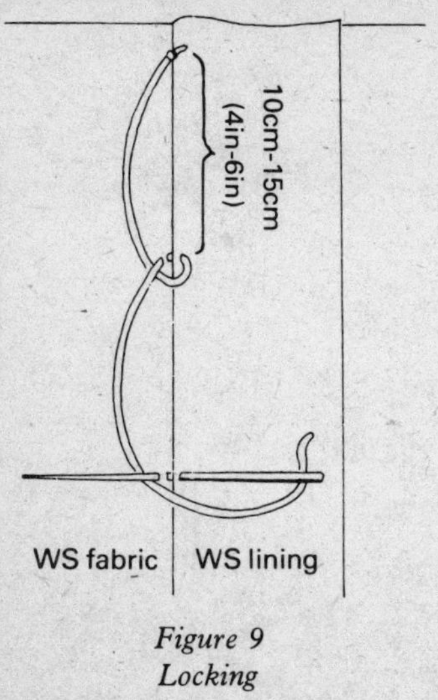

Figure 9
Locking

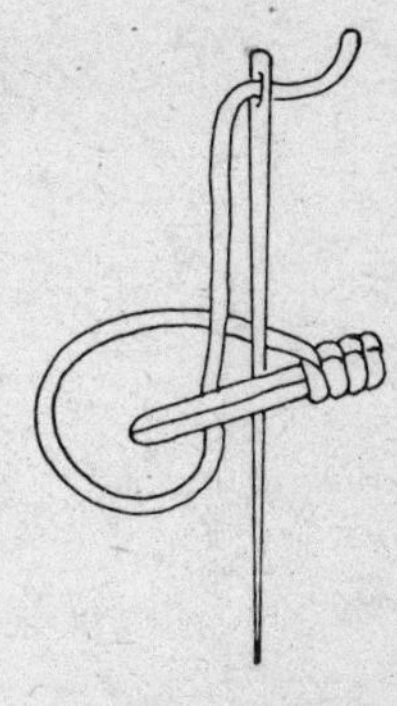

Figure 10
Buttonhole bar

Starting and finishing off

It is usual to start hand-stitching with a knot and finish with two or three back-stitches, running the thread back a little way and cutting it off. However, there are times when other methods are more satisfactory.

Starting

In loosely woven furnishing fabric a knot will sometimes not hold and you can start instead:

1.   by working one or two back stitches;
2.   with an *upholsterers' slipknot*, tucking the loose end under subsequent stitching. This is, in any case, a useful knot to learn as it can be used for buttoning.

Method   (Fig. 11)

1.   Work the first stitch into the fabric and pull it through to leave a short end of about 10–15 cm (4 in–6 in). Hold the two ends of the thread together 6–8 cm (2 in–3 in) away from the stitch.
2.   Bring the shorter end round to form a loop and tuck it twice round into the loop.
3.   Pull the end through to make the knot firm and let it slide up to the stitch.

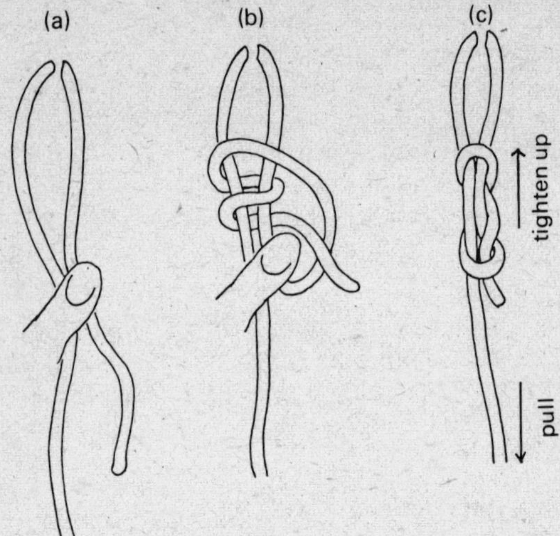

Figure 11   Upholsterers' slipknot

Finishing

Always try to work the back stitches into an inconspicuous part of the work, e.g. the folded edge of the hem rather than the face fabric. Don't cut the thread off close to the stitches but run it back about 2·5 cm (1 in), draw it up slightly so that the fabric puckers and then cut it off close so that the end slips back out of sight when the material is smoothed out.

Using the sewing machine

Use of a sewing machine for soft furnishings is essential as hand-sewing alone is seldom firm enough. To obtain the best use from your particular make of machine it is wise to look out your manual and set aside a few hours to experiment with the various attachments and adjustments. If you are not familiar with any of the sewing machine terms used in this book you will find them in your manual.

The adjustments most often used on a machine involve:

1. stitch length (and width if a zig-zag model);
2. the pressure on the presser-foot;
3. the tension on both upper and lower threads;
4. reverse stitching for starting and finishing.

Look, too, to see if your machine provides any aids to cording (a foot and/or attachment may be supplied).

A special presser-foot is needed for sewing piping – this could double as a zipper foot.

Useful extras are a facility for altering the needle position (sometimes associated with zipper foot/piping foot), some method of immobilising the feed teeth, provision in the spool case for bypassing the tension spring, and a twin needle.

Straight stitching

For seams etc, set the stitch length at 10–12 to the inch (2 or 3 on modern machines) depending on the heaviness of the fabric.

For stay-stitching (a line of straight stitching along the seam line to hold the fabric firm when snipping into the seam allowance) set the stitch at 3 (10 to the inch).

Zig-zag for neatening raw edges

Set the adjustment at the widest setting (usually 4) and shorten stitch length slightly.

Zig-zag for preventing fraying

This is best done on the sewing machine only if you have one that does a 3-step, stepped zig-zag, or wave stitch, as simple zig-zag is apt to pull more threads off the edge. Set at the widest setting and shorten stitch length.

Gathering with the machine

Gathering threads on bulky fabric can be satisfactorily and quickly set in on the machine, but need special treatment as ordinary sewing thread is not strong enough to draw the gathers up. There is a choice of three methods:

1. Wind the spool with heavier thread and adjust the bobbin tension as directed in your manual so that the thread feeds through similarly to normal sewing thread. Set the stitch a little longer than normal and stitch along the seam/gathering line. The heavier thread will be neatly run along the underneath and can be drawn up to produce the gathers.

2. If you have a machine with cording facilities it is possible to run a heavier thread (or cord) along beneath the groove in the foot whilst working zig-zag over it (width 4, stitch length 1–2). Take care not to catch the cord in with the stitching and it will pull up easily to produce gathers.

3. This method uses the twin-needle in conjunction with a cording foot. Instead of working zig-zag over the cord as for (2) the twin needle stitches along either side of it, providing a casing underneath through which the cord can be drawn.

Seams

A simple *flat seam* is machined once on the WS and pressed open. Where the join involves joining two selvedges it is usual to either clip into the selvedges about every 10 cm (4 in) to release the selvedge tension, or to trim them away.

Neatening   Seams on lined articles are not generally neatened. Where a seam involves enclosing piping, or will not be lying flat, it is usual to neaten the raw edges together with overcasting or zig-zag. Work a line of straight machine stitching all round the seam allowance about 13 mm ($\frac{1}{2}$ in) from the seam, trim the raw edge back to this, and immediately overcast or zig-zag.

A *rolled seam* is used for unlined articles, e.g. unlined curtains, especially where a pattern must be matched.

Method for a rolled seam   (*Fig. 12*)

1.   Join two edges together as for a flat seam but with a seam allowance of at least 2 cm ($\frac{3}{4}$ in). Trim back one seam allowance to 6 mm ($\frac{1}{4}$ in).

2.   Fold the wider seam allowance over to make a 6 mm ($\frac{1}{4}$ in) turning and fold over again to meet the stitching line. Either hem the folded edge to the first stitching line by hand, or stitch in place by machine close to the folded edge alongside the first stitching line.

The *welt seam* (or *double machine/machine run* and *fell*) is sometimes used on unlined articles such as bedspreads where fabric widths have to be joined together, and the right and wrong side must look equally neat, but is not suitable for soft bulky fabrics.

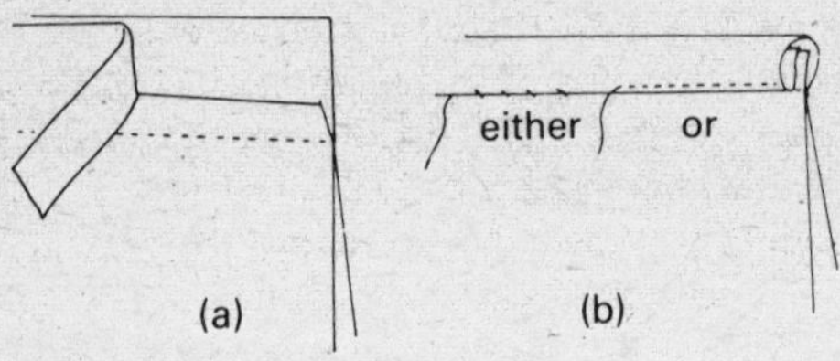

Figure 12   Rolled seam

Method for a welt seam (*Fig. 13*)
Allow a seam allowance of at least 2 cm ($\frac{3}{4}$ in).

1.   Stitch the seam down the seam line on WS. Trim one raw edge back to half the seam allowance.

2.   Fold the wider raw edge over the shorter one and tack down flat to form a hem. Press and machine or hand-hem in place along the hem edge.

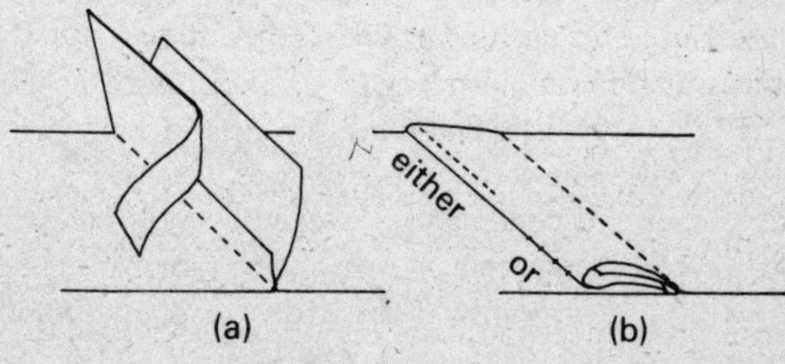

Figure 13   *Welt seam*

4   Measuring, estimating and cutting

Accurate measurement

In soft furnishing measurements are based on the rectangle of cloth into which the pieces of an article must fit. The pieces may have individual shaping such as the curved corners of a cushion, but the starting point is always a rectangle taken over the widest points in each direction (even a circular cushion will have to fit into a square of fabric).

Have ready paper and pencil and a steel rule, and note down the widest measurements across the warp and weft of the fabric on the article, at the same time making it clear which is the widthways, and which the lengthways measurement.

Fig. 14 shows two examples of different-shaped bordered cushions broken down into rectangles. This is the *initial* measurement to which various additions must be made.

Additions to initial measurement

1.   *Seam allowance*

Add at least 13 mm ($\frac{1}{2}$ in) for each seam (*see* Chapter 1).

2.   *Hems and fastenings*

Allowance for these will vary depending on the article and fastening method (*see* Chapter 5 and Part 2).

3.   *Pattern repeats and positioning*

This again will vary with the choice of fabric and the article and may need careful planning and measuring of the exact pattern repeat (*see* Chapter 2).

4.   *Trimmings, pipings etc.*

Extra fabric needs to be allowed for these, and for piping a guide is that 50 cm of fabric will cover 10 m of piping (half a yard of fabric will cover about 10 yd of piping), but often there is sufficient material for piping to be cut from scraps of fabric around the main pieces. For allowance of fabric for frills, pleats etc., *see* Chapter 10.

Note: Measuring for curtains is explained in Chapter 13.

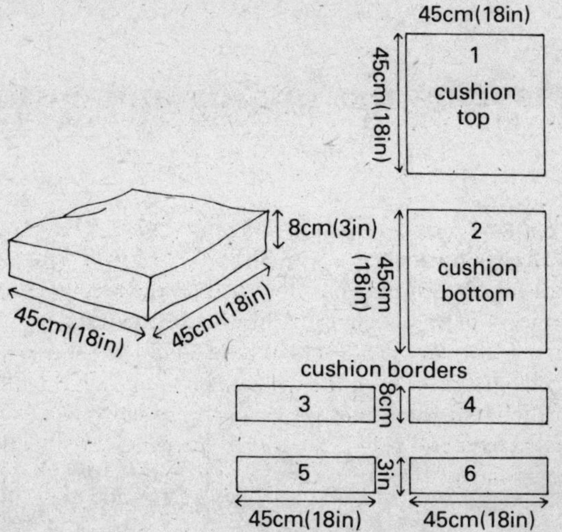

Figure 14a   Measuring a simple, square-bordered cushion comprising six rectangles

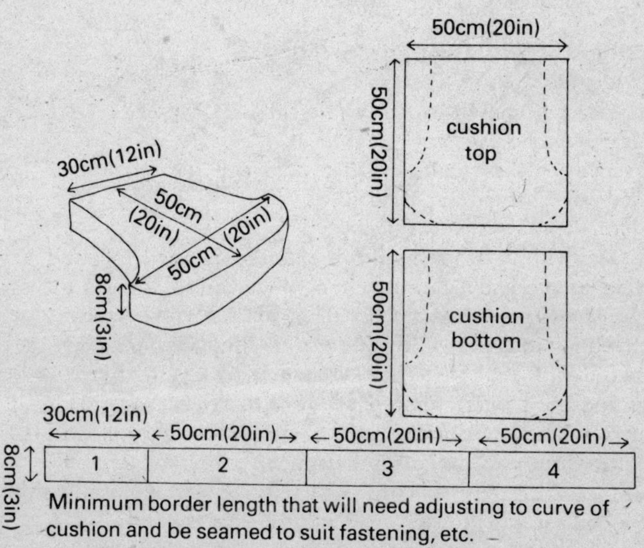

Figure 14b   Measuring a shaped cushion. This is measured in rectangles and fitted after cutting out

To return to the simple bordered cushion (*a*) in Fig. 14, the final 'pattern' would be like Fig. 15.

Top and bottom (2 pieces alike)

$$45 \text{ cm } (+2{\cdot}5 \text{ cm}) \times 45 \text{ cm } (+2{\cdot}5 \text{ cm}) = 47{\cdot}5 \times 47{\cdot}5 \text{ cm}$$
$$(18 \text{ in } (+1 \text{ in}) \times 18 \text{ in } (+ 1 \text{ in}) = 19 \text{ in } \times 19 \text{ in})$$

Four border pieces

$$45 \text{ cm } (+2{\cdot}5 \text{ cm}) \times 8 \text{ cm } (+2{\cdot}5 \text{ cm}) = 47{\cdot}5 \times 10{\cdot}5 \text{ cm}$$
$$(18 \text{ in } (+1 \text{ in}) \times 3 \text{ in } (+1 \text{ in}) = 18 \text{ in } \times 4 \text{ in})$$

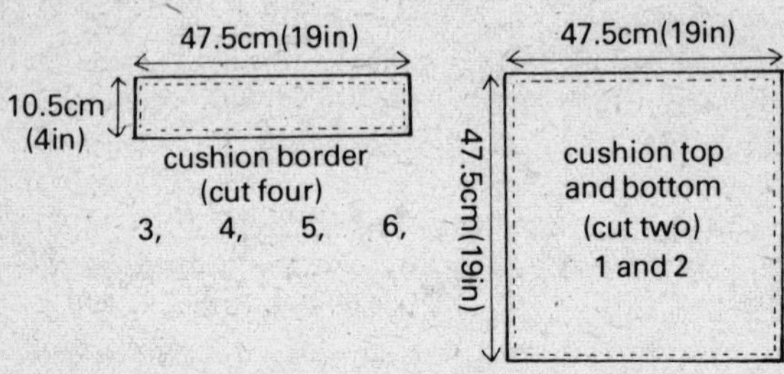

Figure 15   'Pattern' for bordered cushion

(This 'pattern' would be suitable for a cushion without a fastening.) The shaped cushion will be treated similarly, adding a seam allowance all round each rectangle and allowing for piping.

Cutting plan

You have now reached the stage where you can draw out a cutting plan, which will establish both how the pieces will fit into the fabric and how much you will need. It is best to assume that you will be choosing a furnishing fabric with a width of about 122 cm (48 in), so start by drawing a length of fabric and then plan your pieces down it as in Fig. 16.

You can see now quite easily how much plain fabric you need to buy for the rectangular cushion either with or without piping. But if the fabric is patterned you will need to plan your pieces differently. Usually a pattern involves a motif that appears both at regular intervals down the fabric and at least twice across the width, and important parts of any article must be centred on the principal pattern motif. On a bordered cushion this

122cm(48in)

	47.5cm (19in)	47.5cm (19in)
47.5cm(19in)	1	2
10.5cm(4in)	3	4
10.5cm(4in)	5	6
68.5cm(27in)		

fabric needed—70cm(¾yd)

Figure 16a   Planning fabric required for an unpiped cushion

122cm(48in)

47.5cm(19in)	1	2
10.5cm(4in)	3	
10.5cm(4in)	4	
10.5cm(4in)	5	
10.5cm(4in)	6	
89.5cm(35in)		piping

fabric needed—90cm(1yd)

Figure 16b   Planning fabric required for a piped cushion

means centering a motif on the top piece, possibly the bottom piece if you wish to reverse your cushion sometimes, and where the pattern is very pronounced, on each border section too. Depending on where the shop assistant made the cut in the pattern of the fabric, your cutting plan may look like Fig. 17.

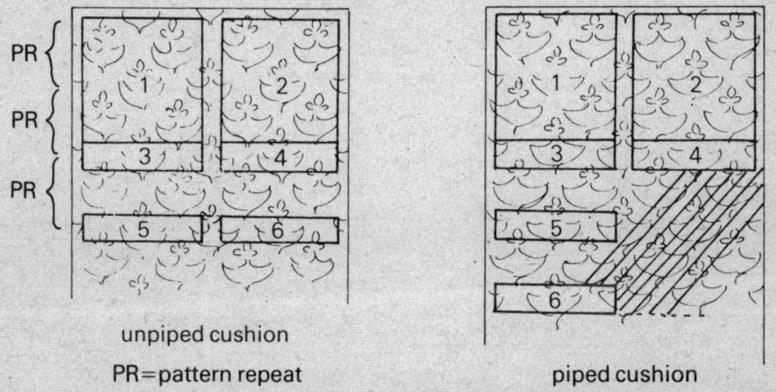

Figure 17   Cutting plan for bordered cushion in patterned fabric

5 Piping (welting)

Piping is used a great deal in soft furnishing: it gives a tailored finish, emphasises the style lines, and takes the brunt of the hard wear on edges. It is true, or course, that this often means the piping wears out before the article, but it can always be cut off and replaced by a cord.

Piping consists of a cord, or core, covered with a casing of fabric. The core most commonly used is a 3-ply twisted cotton cord obtainable in varying thicknesses, Nos 2 or 3 probably being the most popular. Synthetic piping cords are also available but some are inclined to be harder and stiffer than the cotton; however these are less likely to shrink whereas cotton cord will, and it is a wise precaution to pre-shrink it.

Preparing the casing fabric
When working with a woven fabric, the covering for the piping should, ideally, be cut on the cross-way grain. As the strips often have to be cut from odd-shaped scraps left after cutting the main pieces, find the true cross in this way.

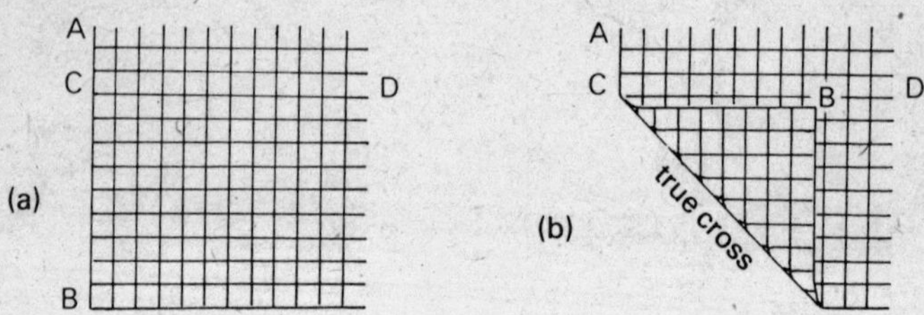

Figure 18   Finding the true cross

Look for woven threads running vertically from A to B and horizontally from C to D. These threads are said to be 'on the grain' (Fig. 18a).

Fold up a corner of the fabric so that the threads from A to B on the corner piece run parallel to those from C to D on the rest of the fabric (Fig. 18b).

Pin the folded corner in place and cut along the folded edge. This cut will be on the *true cross*: if you pull the piece along the cut edge you will find it stretches more than along the grain. This is why crossway strips are used for piping – they will mould and stretch round corners and curves instead of puckering.

Cutting the strips

Crossway strips have to be cut wide enough to wrap round the piping cord and give sufficient allowance beyond the cord for inserting into the seam. The width of the strips will therefore depend on the thickness of the piping cord, and for a No. 2 or 3 cord a strip 4 cm (1½ in) wide is sufficient, giving a seam allowance of 13 mm (½ in).

Several strips joined together may be needed to cover the length of cord required; when using odd scraps, make sure each strip is cut on the same diagonal, i,e SE–NW or SW–NE.

To ensure all the strips are the same width and parallel with the cross-way edge, mark and rule the lines with chalk before cutting them, then trim the top and bottom of each strip along the grain at the same angle as this will help when joining them (Fig. 19).

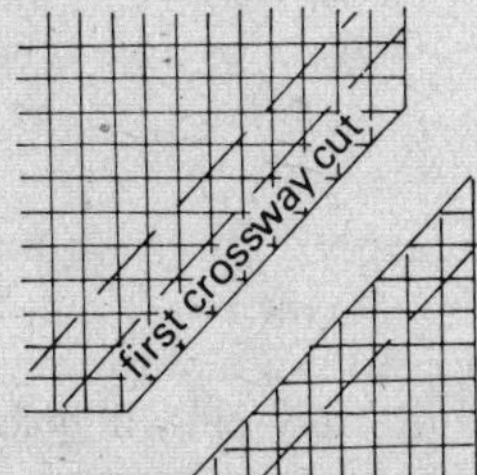

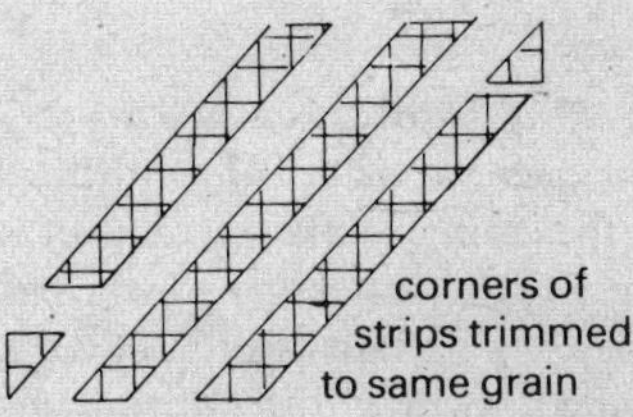

Figure 19

Joining the strips

Crossway strips should always be joined on the straight grain (Fig. 18 A–B, or C–D), and always in the same direction on one article. Seaming on the straight grain ensures a smooth seam; keeping all the joins in the same direction may not seem necessary but so many furnishing fabrics have some kind of stripe produced by thread, print or weave that if you train yourself to keep to this rule you will not find, after inserting the piping, that the colour appears to vary from one joined strip to the next, due to the change of grain.

To join the strips, lay them, RS facing so that their short edges (on the grain) are together: this will mean that the strips lie at right-angles to each other. Shorten stitch slightly and machine the two edges together down the grain line about 7–10 mm ($\frac{1}{4}$ in–$\frac{1}{2}$ in) from the raw edge. Press the seam flat (Fig. 20). Continue joining strips until there is sufficient length to cover the cord.

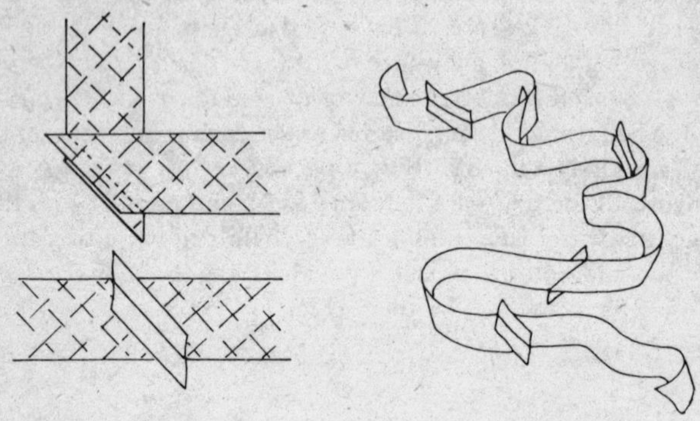

Figure 20   *Joining piping casing*

Preparing piping for insertion

An experienced maker of furnishings would probably at this stage simply wrap the casing round the cord and apply it direct to the article but, for a beginner, it is better to tack the casing in place first. Wrap it round the cord leaving a small amount of cord projecting (a safety-pin will hold the cord and prevent it disappearing up the casing) and tack close to the cord, matching the raw edges of the casing and making sure the fabric WS (where the joins show) is inside (Fig. 21).

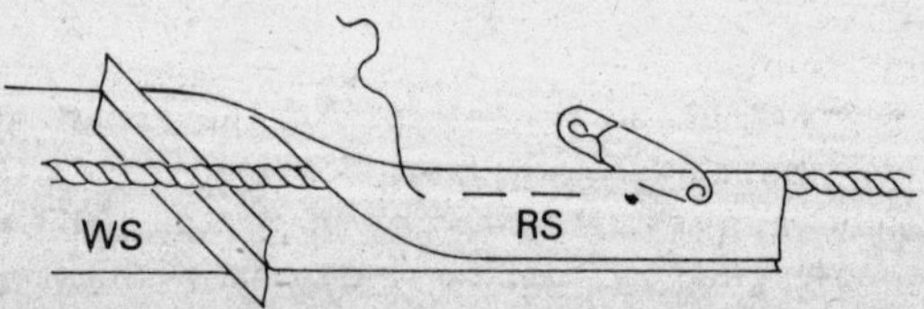

Figure 21   *Preparing piping for insertion*

Inserting the piping
Lay the piece of fabric cut out for the *front* or *top* of the article right side up on a flat surface, and place prepared piping round the edge so that the raw edges of piping and fabric come together. If making, say, a rectangular cushion, arrange the piping so that casing joins do not come at the corners where they will show more.

Tack the piping in place along the previous tack line. If piping has to meet in a final join leave about 7 cm (3 in) untacked each end.

To keep the corners neat and sharp, make a snip into the casing seam allowance so that the piping can be neatly turned at right angles, raw edges matching ready for tacking down the next side. If making a final join, don't cut cord or casing yet (Fig. 22).

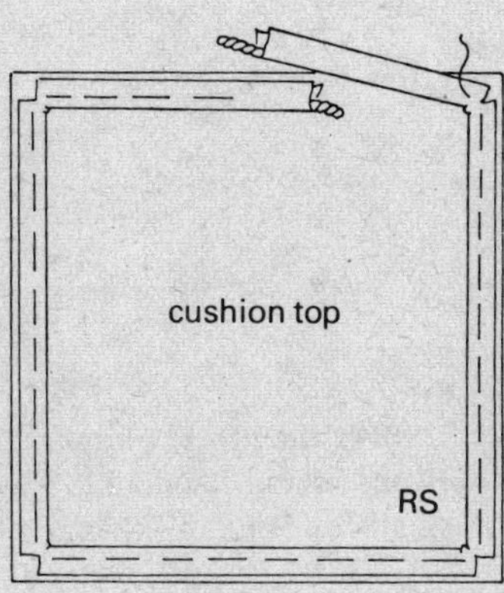

Figure 22   *Inserting piping*

Joining up piping
The casing   This must be done in the same direction as the other joins in the casing. To find the exact place for the join, lap one strip over the other so that they lie flat and insert a central pin. Chalk in a line along the correct grain angle that will allow enough spare fabric for a seam allowance and mark the top of the chalk line with a notch (Fig. 23a).

Remove the central pin and, allowing for a small seam allowance beyond the notch, trim off surplus fabric along the grain (Fig. 23b).

Machine the join by laying the two strips at right angles, RS facing, and raw edges matching. Press the seam open (Fig. 23c).

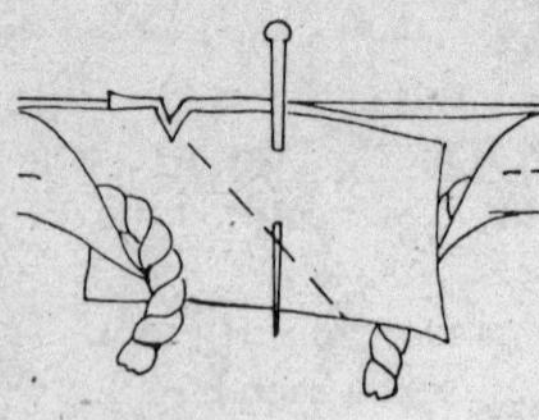

Figure 23a

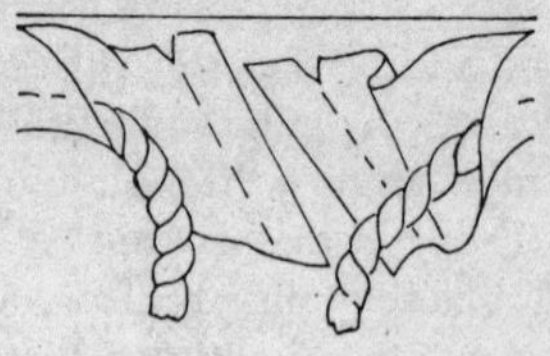

Figure 23b

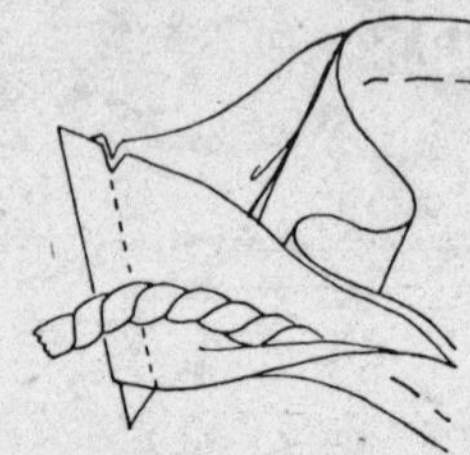

Figure 23c

The cord

Lay one end of the cord over the other, pinning in place centrally. Try to avoid joins in the cord and casing coinciding. Cut away surplus cord to leave 13 mm ($\frac{1}{2}$ in) each side of the pin (giving a 2·5 cm (1 in) overlap) (Fig. 24a).

With needle and thread bind each cord tightly 25 mm (1 in) from the cut end Fig. 24b).

Unravel the ends back to the binding thread so that the three 'ply-s' are separated; then on one cord end cut off two of them, and on the other, one (Fig. 24c).

Twist the remaining three 'ply-s' together so that they resemble the rest of the cord, and wind the thread round them, putting in a few stitches to keep the ends in place (Fig. 24d).

The remainder of the casing can now be wrapped round the joined cord and tacked in place.

Still working with only the one section of your article, machine the piping in place all round where it has been tacked. In order to get as close as possible to the cord, attach a *piping* or *zipper foot* to the machine, and set the stitch length at about 3 (10 to the inch). Keep the corners sharp by swivelling fabric on the needle at the points where the casing is slashed.

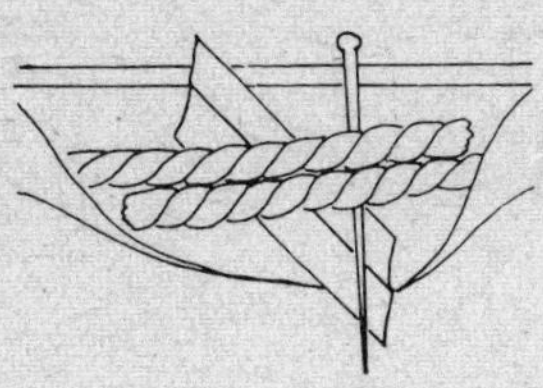

Figure 24a

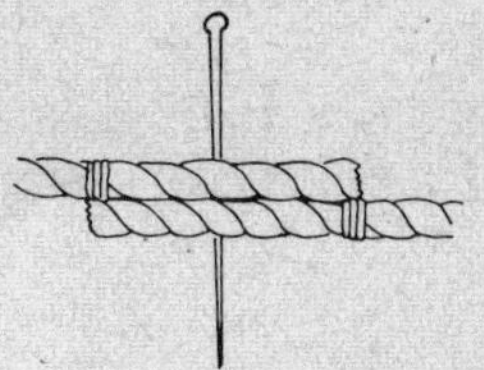

Figure 24b

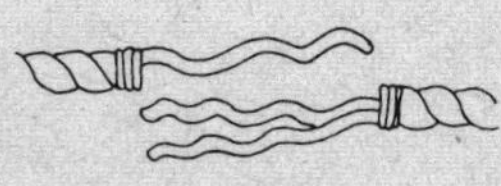

Figure 24c

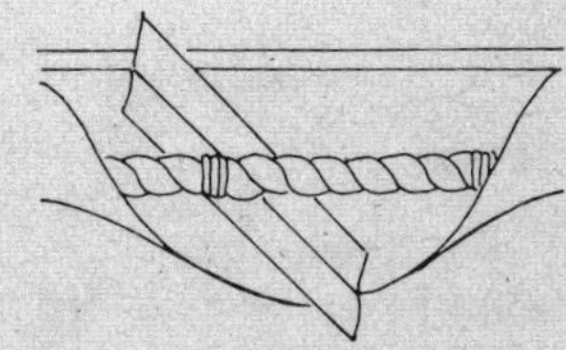

Figure 24d

Note: If a fastening is to be inserted into the seam, this is the stage where it must be considered.

Closing the seam

To do this, place the two halves of the article together on a flat surface so that the WS of the section with the piping is uppermost, RS of each section is facing, and raw edges match. Pin, tack and, using first machine line as a guide, machine round, trying to squeeze even nearer to the piping cord.

Important: If a zip has been inserted, make sure it is undone before closing the seam.

Trim seams to an even width all round, clip across the corner points of the seam allowance, and neaten (*see* Chapter 3).

6   Fastenings and closes

Many soft furnishing items need to have some form of fastening. It is
practicable on a cushion cover that will get very little wear to sew up the
opening (*see* slip-stitch) but usually people prefer to insert a fastening of
some type.

Velcro

This is a 'touch and close' method of gripping two edges together
made up of a double nylon strip, one half of which has a velvet-like surface
whilst the other is covered with a 'pile' of miniature hooks that enmesh
with the velvet instantly on contact, forming a very strong bond. The fact
that the bond is so strong makes Velcro very versatile, enabling it to be used
for a wide variety of purposes such as fixing pelmets, attaching hangings
direct to walls, gripping carpets to floors etc., an added advantage in these
cases being that it is not vital to precisely match one half of the Velcro
to the other. Velcro is available in 15, 20 and 30 mm widths ($\frac{1}{2}$ in, $\frac{3}{4}$ in
and $1\frac{1}{4}$ in) and in a range of colours.

Possible reasons why Velcro might not be suitable for a particular
article are:

1.   it is fairly bulky and makes a rather stiff and heavy join;
2.   because it needs a firm pull to separate the halves, it does involve
some strain on the edges and therefore must be set in very firmly and might
not be ideal for fragile fabric.

Method   (Fig. 25)

1. Preparation

Cut out cushion pieces plus two facing strips for the Velcro wide enough
to give a seam allowance all round the Velcro strip of at least 13 mm ($\frac{1}{2}$ in).

Place together the two sides of the cushion where the opening is to be
and mark its position on the seam edges.

Attach any piping or other trim that needs to be set in to the seam, but
do not join up the cushion seams yet (Fig. 25a).

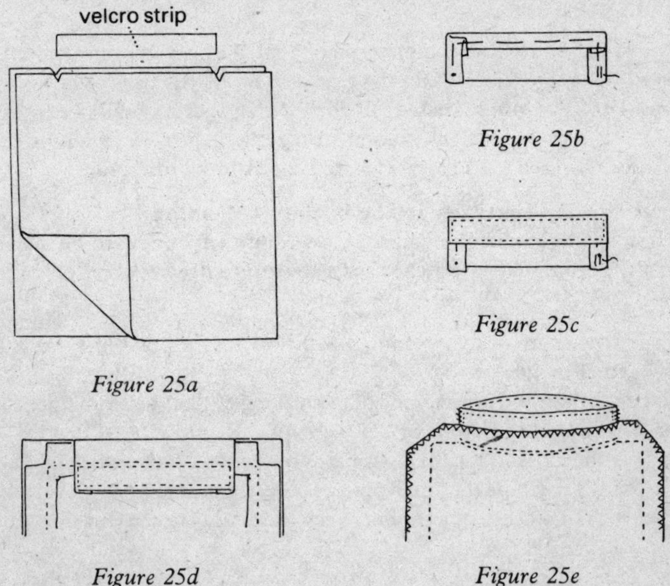

Figure 25a

Figure 25b

Figure 25c

Figure 25d

Figure 25e

2.   Velcro strips

Prepare the fabric facing strips by turning down the seam allowance to WS on all but one long edge. Tack and press (Fig. 25b).

Separate the strip of Velcro and stitch one piece to each of the prepared facing strips, WS together, so that the one remaining raw edge extends for the width of the seam allowance below the Velcro (Fig. 25c). Stitch Velcro about 2 mm (1/10th in) from its outer edge using normal machine presser-foot.

3.   Attaching strips to opening

Position the prepared Velcro strip on each marked edge of opening so that:

(*a*) it is face down on RS of cushion;
(*b*) raw edges of cushion and the facing strip are together;
(*c*) seam allowances match;
Machine strips to cushion along the stitching line (Fig. 25d).

4.   Assembling cushion

Join remaining edges of cushion together starting and finishing at Velcro strip. Oversew the ends of the strips together. Neaten the raw edges, first along strips, then all round the rest of the cushion (Fig. 25e).

Zip fasteners

This is a method of fastening familiar to all. In cushions the zip can be inserted down one side within the seam, or across the back, whichever is appropriate. The latter is easiest to do as the zip can generally be inserted before the cushion sections are joined together. Allow a generous seam allowance (at least 2 cm ($\frac{3}{4}$ in)) where a zip is to be inserted.

Inserting a zip centrally in the back of a cushion

Select a zip slightly shorter than the seam into which it is to be inserted so that the seam may be stitched for a short distance each end of the zip.

Method   (Fig. 26)

1.   Tack the edges of the opening together along the seam line. Press the seam open (Fig. 26a).
2.   Open the zip and lay one side of teeth along WS of the seam line. Tack in place close to the teeth (Fig. 26b).
3.   Close the zip and tack tape in place down the other side (Fig. 26c).
4.   From RS machine the zip in place, taking the stitching down each side parallel with the seam line and square across the zip at each end (Fig. 26d).

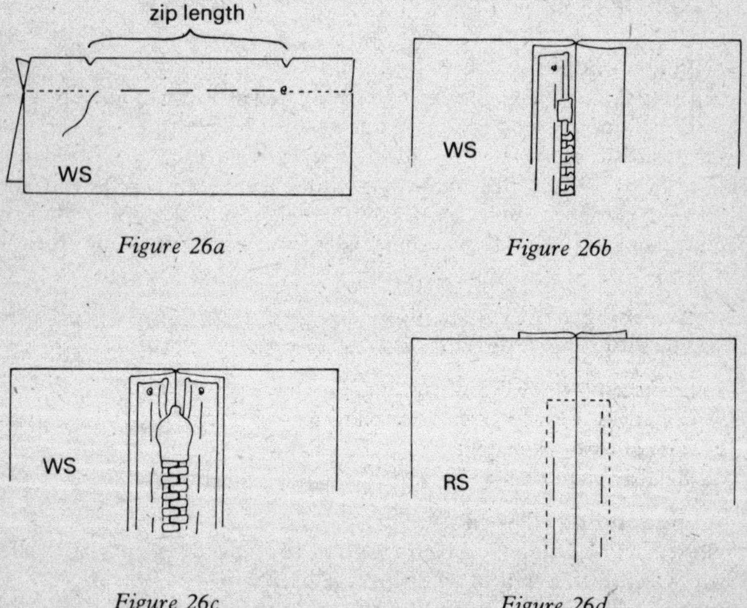

Figure 26a

Figure 26b

Figure 26c

Figure 26d

5.   Trim the raw edges of the seam level with the tape and neaten together. Remove the tacking and work small buttonhole bar stitch across the top of the zip (*see* Fig. 10).

Inserting a zip in the side seam of a cushion

Method   (Fig. 27)
1.   Mark the position of the opening, avoiding taking the zip right up to a corner (Fig. 27a).
2.   Attach any piping etc. to the top section.
3.   Matching the marked opening, place the two sides together and stitch the seam for a *short* distance on either side of the opening. (It is generally sufficient to stitch just to the corners so that the work can be kept flat.)
4.   Undo the zip and on WS place one half of the zip face down over the top (piped) section of the cushion so that the teeth lie along the piping and the tape can be machined on the line holding the piping in place (Fig. 27b). Do up the zip.

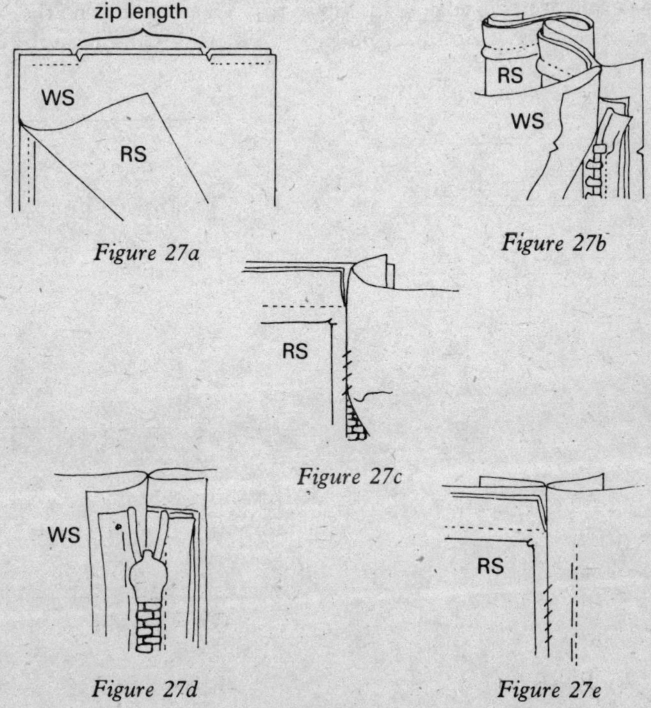

Figure 27a

Figure 27b

Figure 27c

Figure 27d

Figure 27e

5.   From RS firmly tack the edges of the opening together keeping in line with the seam at each end (Fig. 27c).
6.   On WS tack the other half of the zip to the cushion stitching close to the teeth (Fig. 27d).
7.   Using the tacking as a guide line, machine the zip in place from RS, outside tacking, parallel with the seam line (Fig. 27e). Remove the tacking and neaten similarly to central zip.

Inserting a zip down the piped seam of a loose cover

When inserting a zip in these circumstances, a strip of crossway fabric is attached to one side of the zip tape first (the side that will be stitched to the piped side of the opening) to form a facing strip which will neaten the raw edges of the piping and cover. The other side of the opening will only involve a single raw edge so it is not necessary to face this as the edge of the cover and tape can be overcast together to neaten.

Method   (Fig. 28)

1.   Cut a strip of crossway fabric the length of the zip and 5 cm (2 in) wide. Machine it to the edge of the zip so that RS are facing and the raw edge of the crossway strip runs parallel and a short distance from the zip teeth (Fig. 28a).

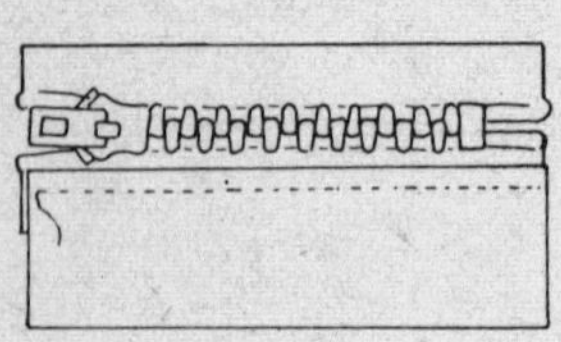

Figure 28a

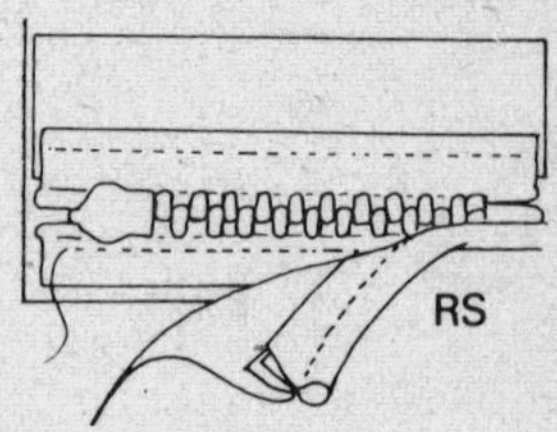

Figure 28b

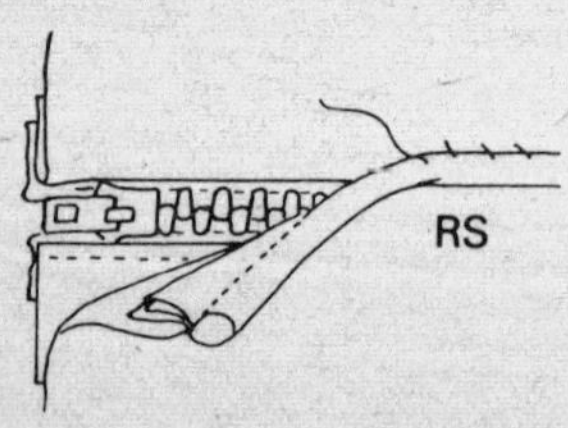

Figure 28c

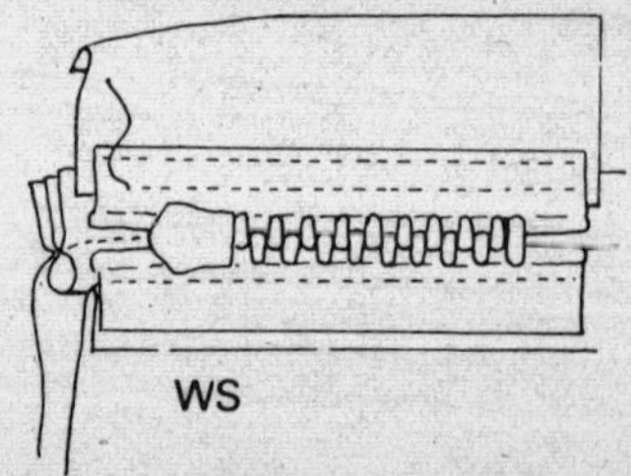

Figure 28d

2.   With RS facing, machine the zip tape without the crossway attached to the unpiped edge of the opening along the seam line, keeping the stitching as close to the teeth as possible without interfering with the running of the zip (Fig. 28b).
3.   On RS, lap the piped edge over the zip to meet the other edge of the opening and catch the edges together with tacking (Fig. 28c).
4.   On WS stitch the zip tape to the seam allowance close to the zip teeth (Fig. 28d).
5.   Turn under the raw edge of the crossway strip and slip-hem in place. Neaten the other side of the zip as for previous zip insertions.

Strap and facing

This is the basis of most fastenings using hooks, studs etc.

A *strap* is a projecting flap of fabric attached to the edge of an opening on to which suitable fastenings may be stitched. When closing the opening, the strap tucks inside to meet its corresponding facing (or strap).

A *facing* is a strip of fabric used to neaten the opening edge, providing support for studs or fastenings. Unlike the strap it does not project beyond the opening edge but folds back to be stitched down on the WS.

It is usual for a strap and facing to be used in conjunction with each other, particularly if the opening edge is shaped, but when providing a fastening method for, say, a straight-sided cushion, two straps may be attached instead. These will show less, as the facing strip is inclined to produce a ridge where it is hemmed down.

A strap and facing is usually applied after the opening position has been marked, piping applied to one side, and a short length of the seam stitched either side of the opening.

The strap – method   (for cushion)   (Fig. 29a, b and c)
Cut a strip of fabric on the straight grain the *length* of the opening plus 2·5 cm (1 in) for turnings, and a *width* of at least 7·5 cm (3 in) giving sufficient for folding double plus a seam allowance (Fig. 29a).

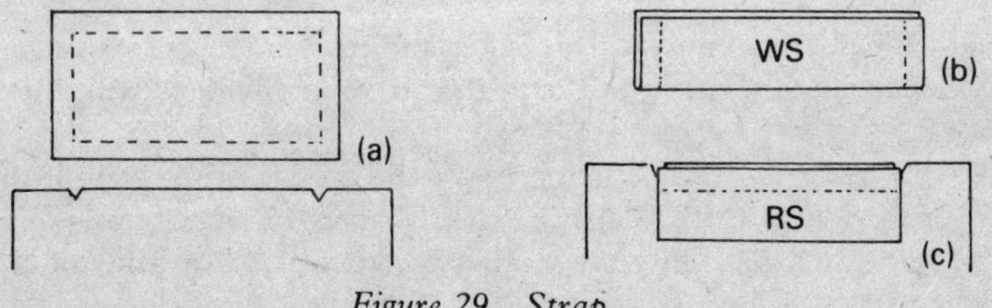

Figure 29   Strap

1. Fold the strip in half lengthwise and stitch across each end on WS with a 13 mm ($\frac{1}{2}$ in) seam (Fig. 29b).
2. Turn to RS and press. Tack the raw edges together.
3. Place in position at the opening, matching the raw edges, and machine in place along the seam line (Fig. 29c). Neaten raw edges.

Note: Where a strap is to be used in conjunction with a facing, the strap is generally applied to the un-piped side of the article.

The facing – method   (Fig. 29 d, e and f)

Cut a strip of fabric about 5 cm (2 in) wide, and the length of the opening plus a turning allowance of 13 mm ($\frac{1}{2}$ in) each end. Where it is to be applied to a shaped edge, use this as a pattern, placing the opening edge face down on the RS of the fabric from which the strip is to be cut (Fig. 29d).

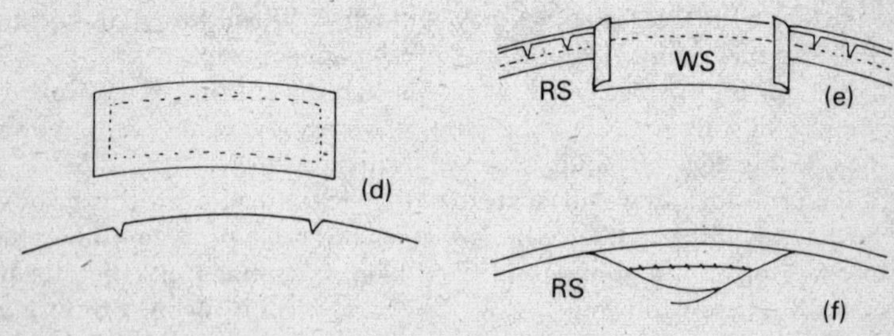

Figure 29   Facing

1. Turn in 13 mm ($\frac{1}{2}$ in) to WS each end of the strip and position at the opening, matching the raw edges (Fig. 29e).
2. Machine the strip in place along the seam line.
3. Finish seaming up the cushion and neaten the raw edges.
4. Turn the facing strip down on the WS, turn under a small hem, and lightly slip-hem it in place (Fig. 29f).
5. Catch each end to the ends of the strap.

Note: When a strap and facing is being applied to, say, a loose cover, there may not be a seam either end, and the above instructions will differ as follows.

  Strap: Step 1. Only stitch across the top edge of the strip if the cover is to have a frill (Valance – *See* Chapter 15) attached.
  Facing: Step 5. Only one end, (sometimes neither end) of the facing is stitched to the strap.

Press studs

These can be bought individually or already attached to a tape. When mounted, as is best, on a strap and facing, or two straps, care needs to be taken that the two halves of the studs come exactly opposite each other. Studs tend to give a rather 'gappy' fastening but are cheap and easy to set in by hand.

Hooks

These are bought with accompanying bars (either straight or looped). For cushion fastening they should be combined with studs as they tend to un-hook themselves; but they come into their own when fastening loose covers, taking the strain of a well-fitted cover better than studs. Hand-worked buttonhole bars look less conspicuous than metal ones but are less strong; a compromise is to work buttonhole stitch over a straight metal bar.

Ties

These have many uses in soft furnishing and can be made of tape or strips of matching fabric (doubled lengthwise, small hems turned in and machined), depending on the purpose for which they are intended. Ties for attaching cushions to chairs are generally set into the cushion seam during making up for extra strength.

Tie-unders are a neat way of keeping loose covers in position and consist of tape threaded through hems (headings) that draw the specially-cut extensions to the outside section of the cover down beneath the chair between the legs. In large chairs, additional loops and ties keep the tie-unders from sagging.

To make a tie-under   (Fig. 30a)
Allow at least 15 cm (6 in) extra fabric. Fig. 30a shows the underside of the chair seat and the position of the tie-under. After cutting and fitting the cover to the chair trim round legs as follows:

1.   At each angle where leg meets chair frame insert a pin, then chalk a line from pin to pin round the leg (Fig. 30b).
2.   Trim away surplus fabric below the chalk line to give a 13 mm ($\frac{1}{2}$ in) turning, cutting up diagonally to the pin for the last 13 mm ($\frac{1}{2}$ in) (Fig. 30c).
3.   Up-end the chair, smooth the fabric over the base, and fold the fabric down to form mitres meeting in the centre.

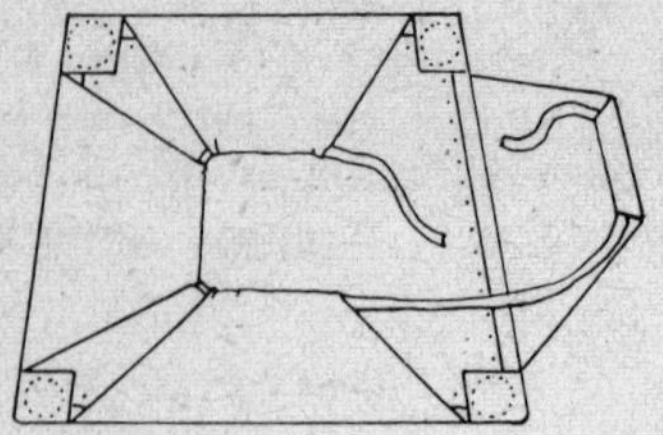

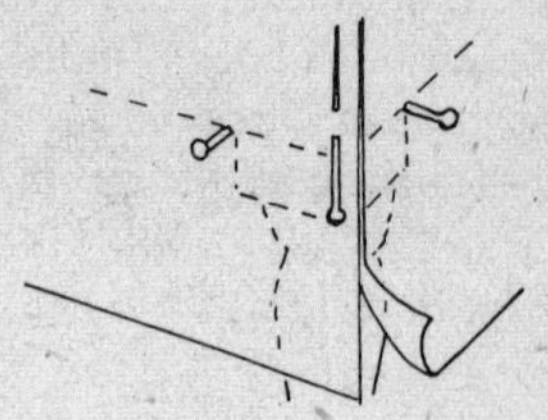

*Figure 30a   Underside of chair
seat to show position of tie-under*

Figure 30b

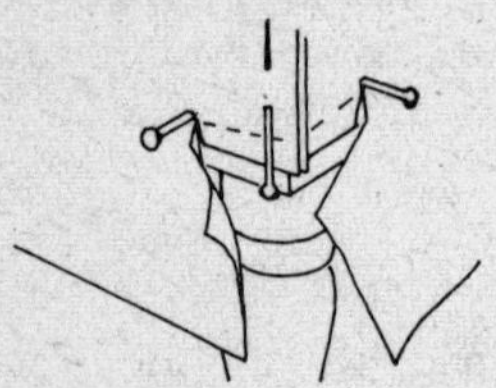

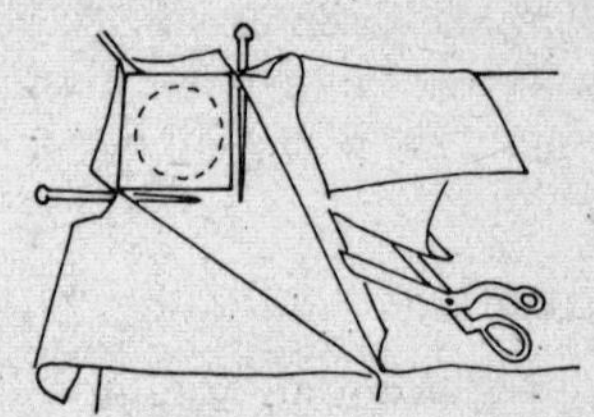

Figure 30c

Figure 30d

4.   Trim away surplus fabric to give a 13 mm ($\frac{1}{2}$ in) turning. This cutting line will meet the corner of the diagonal cut up to the pin. Make sure the tie-under is trimmed to meet, not overlap, under the chair (Fig. 30d).

Note: pins on (b), (c) and (d) are drawn large for clarity.

Neatening the tie-under

The shaped and angled sides of the tie-under are neatened with straight seam-binding; the headings through which the tapes are threaded are formed from simple machined hems.

Apply the binding first, stitching it to the seam line on the RS of the raw edge (Fig. 31a) and then turning the hem down to the WS and edge-stitching (or hand-hemming).

Where the corner forms an acute angle (and the outer edge of the binding will be covering a greater distance than the inner – the first to be stitched) the binding will need to be pleated into a mitre during the first stitching, as follows:

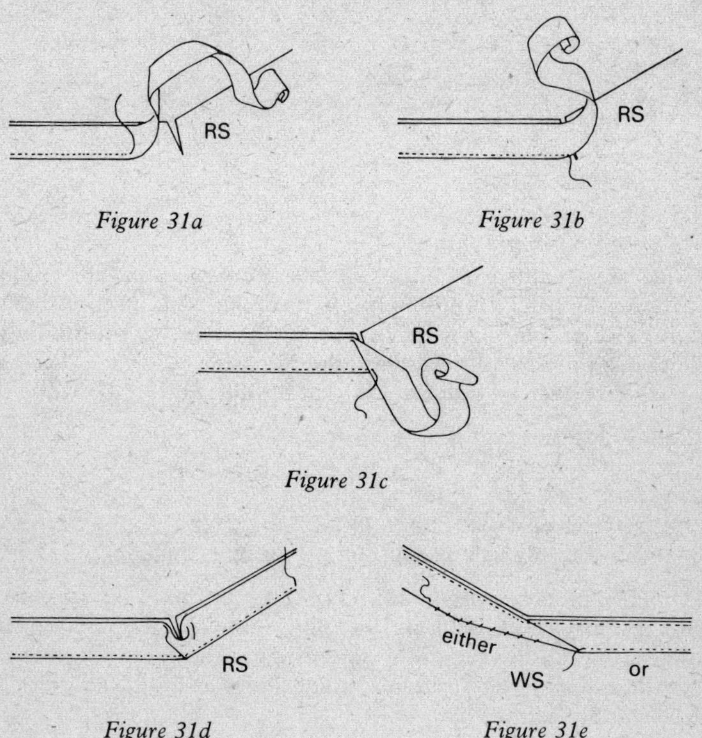

Figure 31a

Figure 31b

Figure 31c

Figure 31d

Figure 31e

1.   Machine up to the corner and raise the presser-foot (Fig. 31b).
2.   Twist the binding over so that it points away, but at a similar angle to that being negotiated (Fig. 31c).
3.   Drop the presser-foot and take the stitiching up to the pleat, dropping the needle into the corner fold of the binding (Fig. 31c).
4.   Lift the presser-foot and swivel the tape round to lie along the stitching line once more. Resume stitching (Fig. 31d).
Fig. 31e shows binding completed on WS.

7 Fillings

A wide range of different fillings is available for cushions and other padded soft furnishings and it is not always easy to decide which to choose. Often it will be a case of buying whatever is easiest to obtain, but where there is a choice this will depend on cost, and the purpose of the article. The main points to consider are whether you want the filling:

1. to be washable;
2. to provide support;
3. to raise the height of, say, a seat;
4. to soften a hard seat;
5. to provide only light padding in, for example, quilting.

Different purposes suggest different fillings, and below is a selection of those that may be available, and the approximate quantities needed for a cushion 50 cm (20 in) square, where appropriate. The three main categories are natural fillings, man-made fillings, and fillings and paddings which can be bought by the yard.

Natural fillings

Down The most expensive type of filling, and used for quilts more than cushions. It is light and soft with good shape retention. The pad case must be of downproof cambric (1 lb (450 g)).

Down and feathers (implying more down than feathers) and *feathers and down* (implying more feathers than down) These fillings are slightly cheaper than down and used for eiderdowns, quilts and cushions. They need a feather-proof fabric (ticking) cover. They are usually sold by the bag – cushion-sized – or already made into cushion pads which sometimes work out as cheap as making the pad oneself.

Feathers Heaviest of this group and popular for cushions. They are often sold as 'curled poultry feathers' in a bag rather than by weight. They need a feather-proof ticking cover (2 lb (1 Kg)).

Note: If you buy striped ticking for the pad, make sure this is not going to show through to the top cover.

All the above fillings should not be regarded as washable.

Kapok is manufactured from the seed covering of a species of the cotton tree imported to this country. It is soft, silky and resilient, but inclined to go into lumps. Because it is moisture resistant it used to be used extensively for life-jackets etc. and could have a use in boat-cushions. No special cover is needed for Kapok. It is sold by the bag.

Flock   Traditionally made from wool waste. A heavy solid filling that packs down to a somewhat unresilient pad. It is most suitable for mattress cushions, pouffes and small pad-seats with a central button to hold the filling. Flock needs stitching through to keep the filling in position if un-buttoned, as otherwise it will move into lumps. It is not washable ($2\frac{1}{2}$–$3\frac{1}{2}$ lb ($1\cdot25$–$1\cdot65$ Kg) depending on depth of cushion).

Loose man-made fibre fillings

A wide range of these have come on the market under various brand names. Some state an actual fibre composition but others appear to be made from waste man-made fibres from various sources. All are washable, clean, moth and mildew resistant, and need no special cover to the pad. They vary in weight and price and some behave like Kapok, going into lumps. Tease fibres out well as you fill the pad.

Loose Polyester is often sold under brand names such as Terylene or Dacron. It is soft, light and dries quickly if washed. The most expensive filling of this group. It does not go lumpy and has good shape retention (1 lb) (450 Kg)).

Loose Acrylic   Slightly cheaper and sometimes goes into lumps if composed of waste fibres. It needs teasing out well (1 lb) (450g)).

Foam

Latex foam   Not so easy to obtain as it is a product of natural rubber. It is very soft and resilient but will perish and disintegrate with prolonged use. It is available as moulded shapes with cavities. It is used widely for loose seats on fireside chairs and suites but is rather expensive.

Polyether foam   Sold in sheet form and moulded shapes, in a wide variety of thicknesses, grades and densities. It is inclined to be a bit 'unsympathetic' as a cushion filling as it does not mould to the shape of a chair. It is improved by wrapping in one or more layers of wadding and inserting in a scrim or cheese-cloth casing, which incidentally will help it to wear longer.

Latex and polyether foam crumbs or chips   These are sold by the bag for cushion fillings, the Latex being the softer. If the chips are too large they are apt to show as lumps through the cover, but they are clean, washable and need no special cover.

Bonded chipfoam   Polyether foam chips bonded into sheet form and very durable, and firm. Good for church kneelers.

Polystyrene granules (*beads*)   These have a limited use for floor cushions, 'sag-bags', and cushions for pets. They are best put first in a strong calico lining and then into a top cover. They are available by mail order and sold in cartons of 12 cu ft sufficient for a chair-sized bag.

Springing

Often a cushion is made up of a spring unit covered in thick wadding inserted into the cover.

Spring units are of two kinds: those made up of light-gauge springs joined together with spiral wire and generally encircled by a heavy-gauge wire edging to produce the cushion shape; and those made up of light individual springs pocketed in calico or scrim which are stitched together in rows to build up the size of the cushion.

In the first type of unit, if a spring breaks poking through the cover, little can be done, unless the manufacturer will replace the whole unit, except substitute a foam filling. However, if the latter gets damaged it is sometimes possible to replace a spring or shift them round so that the springs getting the least wear are moved into the worn springs' place.

When renovating a spring unit, it needs to be wrapped in several thicknesses of thick upholstery wadding before inserting into the cover. This is easier to do if the wrapped unit is put first into an inner cover of cheap cotton made up with a *very wide* opening that need only be roughly hand-stitched up before the whole is placed in the top cover. This cotton cover ensures that the wadding stays smoothly in position.

Fillings and padding sold by the metre (yard)

There are a wide range of these suitable for padding quilts etc. and for interlinings. They are available in various thicknesses dependent on the depth of padding needed.

Sheet or skin wadding

This comes in natural or man-made fibres and can sometimes be used as a cushion filling if layered. Resilience and depth varies with the fibre, as does washability.

Polyester   Often sold as Terylene or Dacron. The most expensive of the group and also the most springy, sometimes being sold in a triple-layered depth ideal for cushions or eiderdowns. It is less suitable for traditional quilting as its springiness makes it difficult to handle. It is washable and usually sold on a 1 m (39 in) width roll.

Acrylic   Often sold as Courtelle. Cheaper than polyester but excellent quilt filling – springy and soft but not usually so thick (1 m (39 in) width roll).

Triacetate   Tricel wadding is sometimes available. It is a flatter, less springy wadding, ideal as a washable alternative to cotton skin wadding (sometimes 45 cm (18 in) wide).

Cotton (skin) wadding is the cheapest of the sheet waddings. It tends to break up when washed. (usually 45 cm (18 in) wide but will open out to a thin double-width).

Linterfelt   A thick upholstery wadding composed of a flock-like padding sold on the roll backed by crepe paper and available from upholstery suppliers when it is often sold by weight rather than length. It is needed for wrapping springs and spring units, but can be used in place of flock for pad-seats.

Woven knitted paddings and interlinings
Bump   Traditionally used as a curtain interlining but also good as a light padding. Looks like flannelette blanket (which can be used as a substitute). It will sometimes shrink if washed (122 cm (48 in) wide).

Flat domette   Similar to bump but lighter, and used in similar circumstances for giving light padding to small articles. It may shrink (91 cm (36 in) wide).

Fluffy/fleecy domette   Fluffy fabric of knitted construction with a raised surface on one side. It is lightweight and ideal when quilting or padding small articles (133 cm (52 in) wide).

8   Channelling

When a loose filling is used in a cushion pad above a certain size it will tend to shift about unless it is filled very full indeed. In soft pillow cushions this does not always matter, but in bordered cushions, especially on chair seats, a technique called channelling is used to make walls inside the pad which contain the filling and ensure an even distribution.

To make a 2-walled channelled cushion pad for a bordered cushion

Pad size – 50 cm (20 in – square with a 10 cm (4 in) border)
Seam allowance – 15 mm ($\frac{1}{2}$ in)

Method   (Fig. 32)
Cut pieces as follows:
Top and bottom (A and B) 53 cm (21 in) × 53 cm (21 in).
4 border pieces (C, D, E, F) 53 cm (21 in) × 13 cm (5 in).
2 wall pieces (G, H) 53 cm (21 in) long × 13 cm (5 in) each end raised to about 16 cm (6$\frac{1}{2}$ in) in centre.

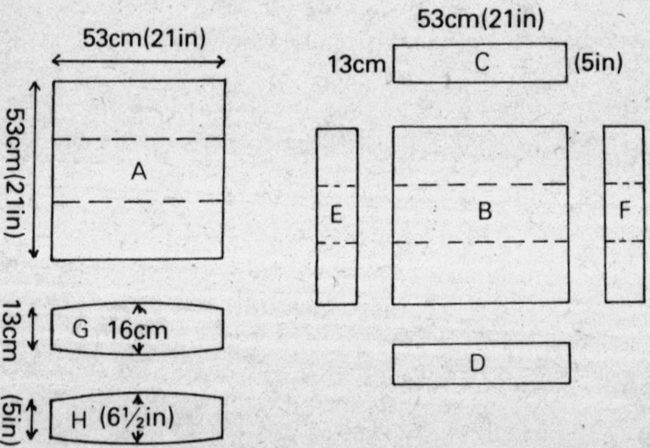

Figure 32

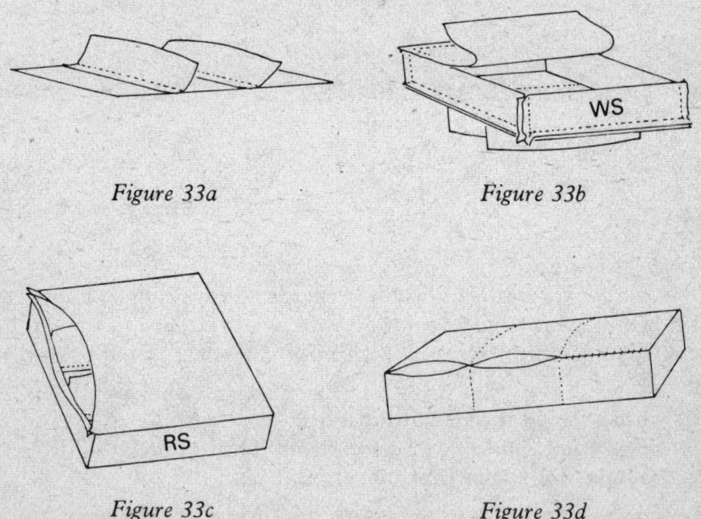

Figure 33a

Figure 33b

Figure 33c

Figure 33d

1. On the top and bottom pieces mark the position of the walls on WS. Lay border strips alongside and mark the wall positions similarly. Machine stitch one long side of a wall to each marked position on the pad top leaving 15 mm ($\frac{1}{2}$ in) each end unstitched (Fig. 33a).
2. Seam border to pad top all round on WS. Similarly, seam pad bottom to border, leaving one of the marked sides open. Turn through to RS (Fig. 33b).
3. Through opening, pin and machine the walls to the bottom of the pad along marked positions (Fig. 33c).
4. Attach the walls to the borders. It is easier to do this by hand and can be omitted altogether. Fill each section and stitch up the opening (Fig. 33d).

Note: This same channelling principle is applied to the making of continental quilts, and is the reason why they are warmer than eiderdowns. Usually five to seven narrow walls are inserted, and these may be attached to top and bottom before the quilt is stitched round the edge because of the difficulty of reaching inside such a large article.

9 Gathers and pleats

Gathers

1. *Fullness allowances*   The average allowance for gathers is *one and a half times the finished length*, or half as much again. For example, the gathered frill of a dressing table 92 cm (3 ft) wide would be cut 138 cm (4 ft 6 in) wide (plus turnings). Occasions when this allowance would be increased are:

(*a*) when a frill goes round a corner, e.g. of a cushion.
(*b*) on very fine fabrics, e.g. net curtains, when as much as two and a half to three times fullness can be allowed.

2. *Setting in gathers*   (*see also* Chapter 3) Divide the ungathered frill, and the edge to which it is to be attached, into the same number of equal parts, and then draw up the gathers, pinning and tacking a section at a time so as to distribute the fullness evenly.

Pleats

There are four basic types of pleat used in soft furnishing – *box*, *inverted*, *knife* and *pinch* (also called Triple, French and Goblet). The easiest way to understand them is to fold them on a strip of paper:

1. Box pleat   (Fig. 34 a and b)

This can be a close pleat or one with a space between. To fold a close 5 cm (2 in) box pleat mark a strip of paper every 5 cm (2 in) labelling the marks A, B, C etc. Fold B to A and C to D, E to D and F to G and so on. The paper strip will now only measure a third of its original length and looked at end on will have formed a triple width of paper. Therefore the *allowance* needed for *close pleating* is *three times* the finished length.

Box pleat and space

Prepare the paper strip as before but this time fold B to A and C to D, F to E and G to H etc. Looking at this pleating end on you will see that the layers alternate between triple and single sections equivalent to a double

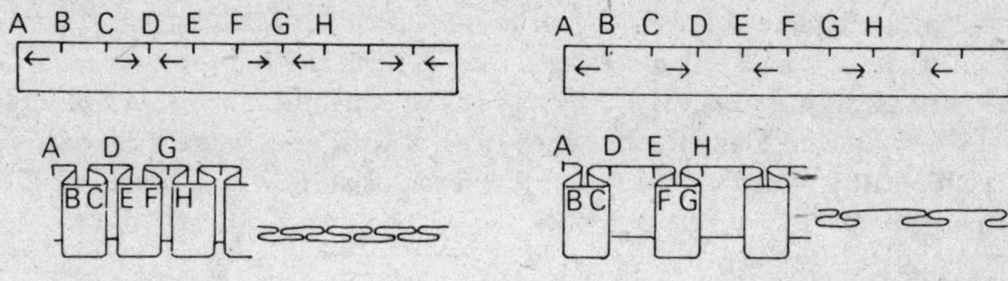

Figure 34a   Box pleat   Figure 34b   Box pleat and space

thickness all along, so the *allowance* needed for *equal pleat and space* is *double* the finished length.

2.   Knife pleats   (Fig. 34 c and d)

For close knife-pleating, mark out the strip in alternate sections of 5 cm (2 in) and 10 cm (4 in) and label A, B, C, D etc. Fold B to C, D to E, F to G etc. This, being *close pleating*, will again need *triple fullness*.

A knife pleat and space will give the appearance of a double-width pleat from the front. Mark out in 10 cm (4 in) divisions and fold B to C, D to E, F to G etc. This will, of course, *need double fullness*.

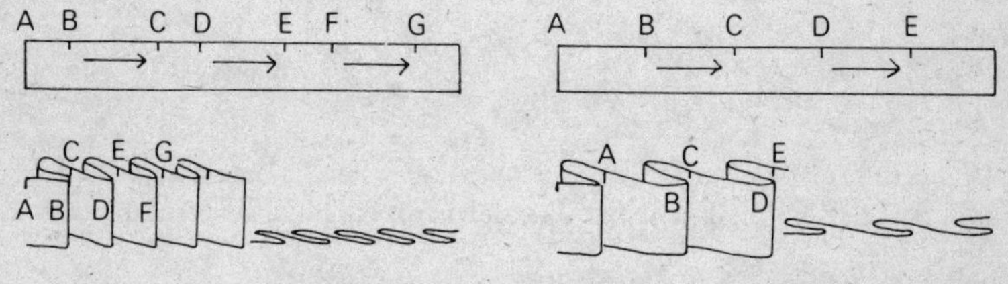

Figure 34c   Knife pleat   Figure 34d   Knife pleat and space

3.   Inverted pleats

An inverted pleat is really the opposite side of a box pleat and can be treated as above. However, more often inverted pleats are used singly at corners of, e.g. bed valances or 'frills' of loose covers, and in this case a deep pleat taking about 30 cm (12 in) into each side of the pleat is usual.

4.   Pinch pleats   (Triple, French, Goblet)   (Fig. 34 e to h)

This is a type of pleat only suited to an unattached heading (one that is not set into a seam) as the top of the pleat is open to form double or triple pleats (French) or opened out and padded lightly (Goblet). The pleats are formed after the article has been neatened along the top edge, and to make the pleats crisper a strip of interlining – either special curtain heading buckram or Vilene – is inserted to the depth of the pleat.

The pleats are planned on the basis of an equal pleat and space (double fullness) and to look effective they need at least 10–15 cm (4 in–6 in) in each pleat; it is usual to start and finish the pleating with a space or part-space.

Method

For a 15 cm (6 in) pleat and space mark off the heading in 15 cm (6 in) sections but start with a 7·5 cm (3 in) space, labelling each mark A, B, C etc. (Fig. 34e).

1. Pin A to B, C to D, E to F etc. and from each pinned point stitch down for the depth of the pleat (usually about 7·5 cm (3 in)) either by hand or machine (Fig. 34f).

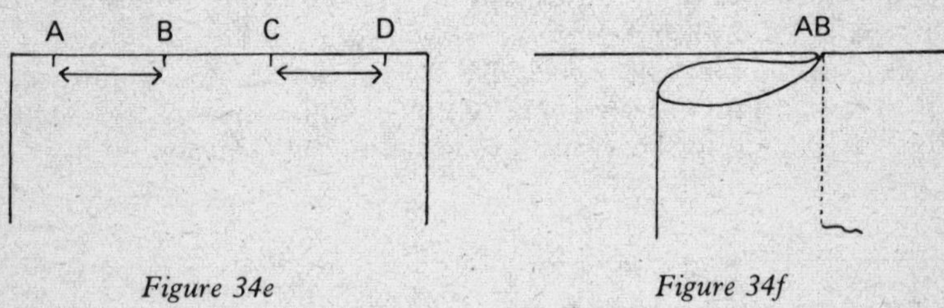

Figure 34e   Figure 34f

2. Form the pleats into three (or two) equal small pleats and at the base, where the stitching finished, stab-stitch across to hold the pleat in position (Fig. 34g).
3. Open the top of the pleat and oversew to the top of the curtain 2 cm ($\frac{3}{4}$ in) from stitching. (Goblet pleats are padded lightly with tissue paper) (Fig 34h).

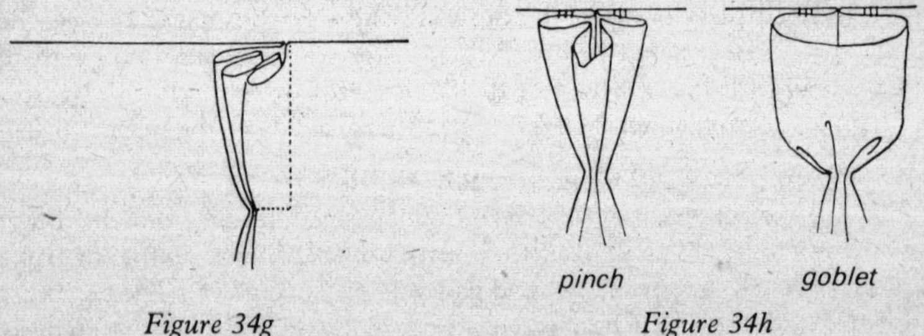

Figure 34g   Figure 34h
Finished pinch and goblet pleats

5. Pencil cartridge pleats

This is a popular type of deep heading for curtains and is really not a pleat at all, but a form of gathering in which the gathering cords running in and out of the heading tape are matched over each other vertically so that when the cords are drawn up a row of parallel folds are formed. It is possible to form this type of heading by hand without a commercial tape, but it is more usual, and certainly easier, to use one of a number of commercial tapes sold for this kind of heading, such as Rufflette Regis which has a special reinforcing thread running through the weave of the tape to keep the pleats crisp. Because the gathering cords need to be drawn up closely to form this heading triple fullness allowance is needed.

10 Mitres

A mitre is the angle at which two sides meet involving a turning or border at a corner. When the turning or border is of equal width down each side on a right-angled corner the angle of the mitre will be 45°, but if this is not the case the angle will vary.

The mitres used most in soft furnishings are:

1. Hem mitres, formed when the hem turns a corner.
2. Flat mitres formed when a flat strip (e.g. round the outer edge of a double eiderdown) turns a corner.
3. Double mitres formed when a double strip is applied which turns a corner (e.g. the contrast band round the hem of a curtain).

1. Hem mitre   (Fig. 35)

When making lined curtains, the purpose of the corner mitre on the face fabric is to control the fabric bulk without cutting any away and at the same time exactly meet the corner of the lining.

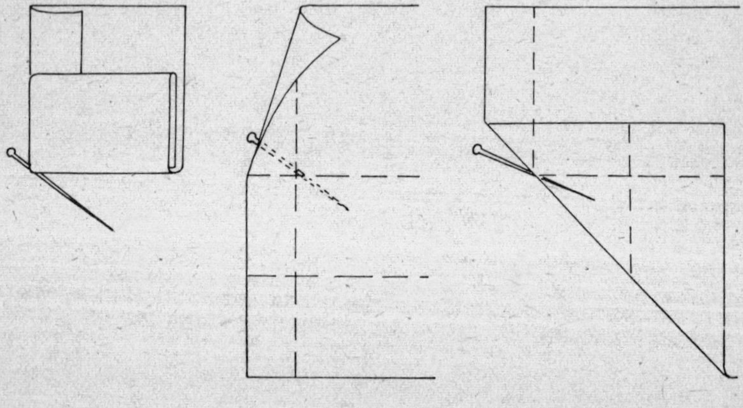

Figure 35a   Figure 35b   Figure 35c

Method for 45° mitre

1.   Turn up hems to finished positions, pressing in crease marks, and mark corners with a pin (Fig. 35a).

2.   Unfold hems to show crease marks (Fig. 35b).

3.   Refold corner diagonally so that the pin comes on the folded edge and crease marks are lined up over each other (Fig. 35c).

4.   Fold over the first side hem and then the lower hem to form the mitre (Fig. 35d and e).

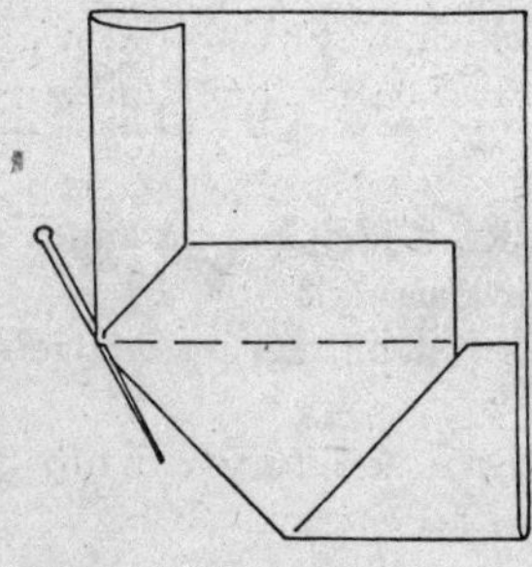

Figure 35d

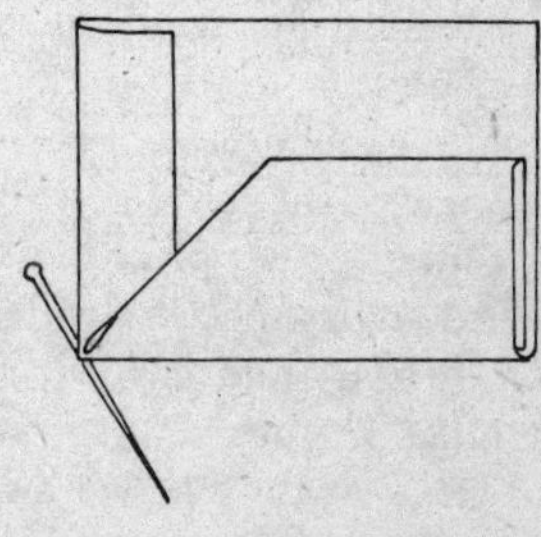

Figure 35e

2.   Flat mitre (45°)   (Fig. 36)

Method

1.   Cut strips required adding sufficient allowance not only for the turnings but also to travel round the *outside* edge of the strip when it turns the corner.

2.   Measure the length of the inner edge to which the strip is to be applied and mark this on the strip within the seam allowance. From this point mark out a 45° angle to the outer edge of the strip (Fig. 36a).

3.   Place the marked edges of the two strips together, RS facing, and machine along the angle between the turning allowances. Trim back the seam to 13 mm ($\frac{1}{2}$ in) and press open (Fig. 36b).

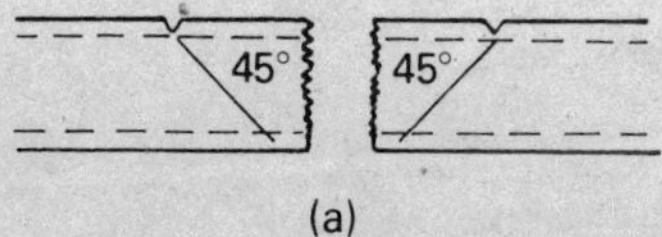

(a)

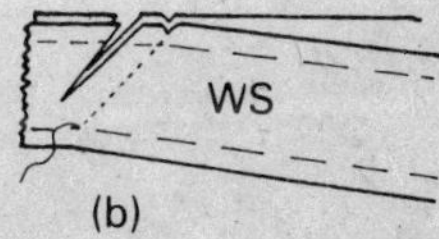

(b)

Figure 36

3.   **Double mitre**   (Fig. 37)

Method

1.   Cut strips long enough either to (A) go along each edge of the article, or (B) go completely round the article, in either case adding sufficient for mitring (width of border plus turnings). The width of the strips should be twice the finished width plus a double turning allowance, e.g. a 2·5 cm (1 in) border needs a strip 7·5 cm (3 in) wide.
2.   Fold the strips in half lengthwise, marking the fold position, and mark the turning allowance down each side (stitching line).
3.   Measure the length of the edge to which the strip is to be attached and mark this on the stitching line.
4.   From the measured positions mark a 45° mitre which will meet in a 90° angle at the fold line (Fig. 37a).
5.   Either for (A) place two strips together, RS facing, and machine two marked angles together within the seam allowance.
   Or for (B) fold strip over at mitre point and machine along mitre line (Fig. 37b or c).
6.   Trim surplus fabric away, press seam flat and turn strip to RS (Fig. 37d).

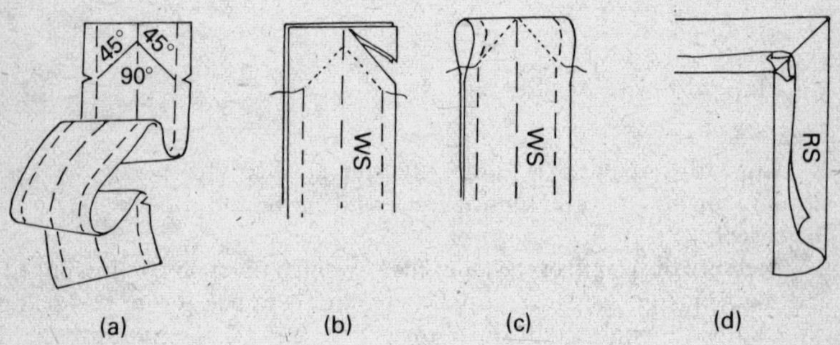

Figure 37

11   Cords, gimps, braids and trims

A wide variety of these is available ready-made, and can be attached by hand or machine. Here is some general advice.

Braids and gimps should be mitred at the corners to produce a neat turn. If applying them to an article that is to be lined, or along a hem edge, apply the trim *before* attaching the lining or turning up the hem.

Be careful not to pull the trim whilst applying it or it will pucker the fabric.

Many cords and gimps fray or unravel quickly. It is wise to seal the end quickly with either a few drops of clear adhesive or sellotape. When cutting off a length of gimp or cord, first wrap sellotape round the part to be cut and then cut centrally through it.

Handling cords

One of the chief problems when applying cord round an article is how to handle the inevitable join without it showing too much. Here are some suggestions:

1.   Where possible, overlap the ends slightly and tuck both ends into the seam before stitching the seam up firmly. In rectangular articles the join will show less on a corner than as a lump mid-seam.
2.   If applying cord to a cushion it is possible to make a decorative loop at each corner, incorporating the join into one of these.

Attaching cord   (Fig. 38)

Cord should not be attached by taking a stitch 'over and over' the cord. The correct method gives an invisible stitch that will hold the cord firmly, keeping the thread between the ply's.

Method   (Fig. 38)

1.   Take a stitch in the fabric beneath where the cord is to lie.
2.   Slant the needle up through 2 or 3 ply's and draw the thread through (Fig. 38a).
3.   Stab the needle straight back down (Fig. 38b).

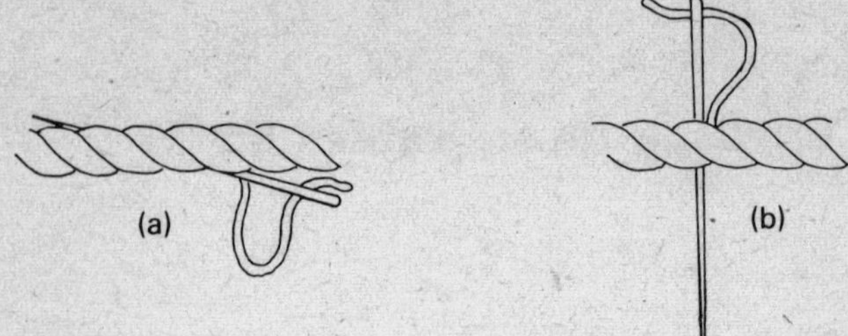

Figure 38   Attaching cord

Some alternative trims

It is not always necessary to buy expensive trimmings as there are many ways in which you can produce your own:

1.   Apply strips of patterned or contrasting fabric, either flat or in the form of a rouche (gathered each side).
2.   Set in or apply a gathered or pleated frill of matching or contrasting fabric.
3.   Bands of simple embroidery stitches are a good substitute for braid.
4.   Edges of loosely woven fabric can be frayed out to form a fringe.
5.   Plaits can be formed of toning knitting or rug wool, or from threads withdrawn from the fabric.
6.   Piping cord (which dyes well) can be held in place (couched) decoratively by selecting a simple embroidery stitch and working it over the cord, catching it to the fabric at spaced intervals.

PART 2

Introduction

In this section you have the opportunity to combine the skills learnt in Part 1 in the making of various articles of soft furnishing.

For example, if you are a beginner, you could start by making the first article in Part 2, a simple pillow cushion, and refer back to: Chapter 1 to check you have all the necessary equipment; Chapter 2 to select a suitable fabric; Chapter 3 for all the stitches and seam finishes you will need; Chapter 4 to help you decide how much fabric you will need and how to cut it economically; Chapter 5 to make a neat piping round your cushion; Chapter 6 to insert the fastener; Chapter 7 to help you choose a filling and cover for the pad.

These same skills can be transferred to a variety of different sizes and shapes of cushion besides the one described in detail.

This principle applies to all the articles described in the following section. You will find that some skills are used over and over again whatever the article, always combined with other skills that arise only for specific articles, but with the confidence gained by repetition you will soon find yourself able to tackle any soft furnishing item.

12   Cushions

The pad   (*See Chapter* 7)
It is quite possible to make a wholly washable cushion by simply filling a
washable cover with a washable filling and sewing it up; however it is more
usual to make a separate pad for the filling, over which a removable cover
is fitted.

The pad should always be slightly *larger* than the cover to ensure a well-
filled appearance, a guide being the addition of about 2.5 cm (1 in) on a
50 cm (20 in) cushion.

The pad is made the same shape as the cushion and is cut with 13 mm
($\frac{1}{2}$ in) turnings. For additional strength, a double line of machining can be
worked round the seam (which doesn't need to be neatened), and the stitch
length shortened slightly. Always leave a generous opening for inserting
the filling.

Filling the pad
Kapok and loose synthetic fillings need picking over to tease out any lumps
before placing in handfuls in the pad cover. As fluff will rise, tie a scarf
over your nose if you are sensitive to it.

Loose foam can be messy and needs transferring over a tray or sheet to
catch and save the bits.

Down and feathers are very messy indeed and should be transferred
outside on a still day or in a small, easily-cleaned room. They are best
transferred from one fabric bag to another by making an opening in each
and sewing the two together, then patting the filling through to the new
cover. If, however, they are supplied in a plastic bag, there is no alternative
to shaking them from the bag into the cover.

After filling the pad, oversew or machine the opening up firmly. If using
a *solid foam shape* make sure the cover is a good fit and leave a generous
opening or it will split when inserting the foam. A layer of wadding can
be eased in between the cover and the foam to soften the shape and prolong
the life of the foam. The corner angles of the foam shape can be further
softened by trimming them away with scissors.

Making cushions

1. A pillow cushion

In plain fabric with piped edge and Velcro fastening, size 25 cm × 35 cm (10 in × 14 in).

Materials (*see* cutting plan Fig. 39)

Cover
32.5 cm (13 in) of 122 cm (48 in) fabric
25 cm (10 in) of 25 mm (1 in) Velcro
130 cm (1½ yd) of Piping cord
Sewing thread

Pad
30 cm (12 in) of 91 cm (36 in) fabric
12 oz approx of synthetic filling

Cutting plan **(Fig. 39)**

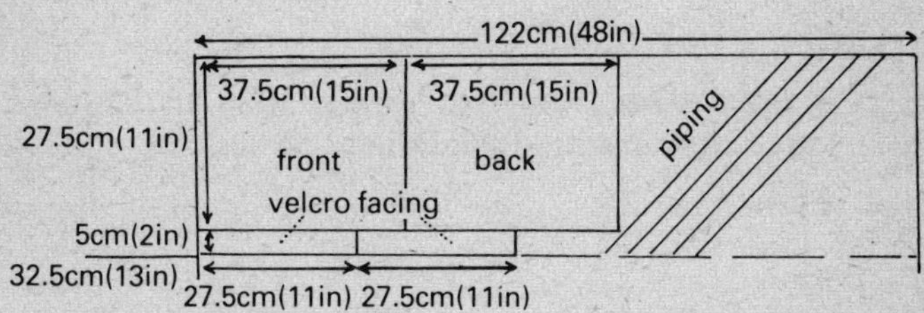

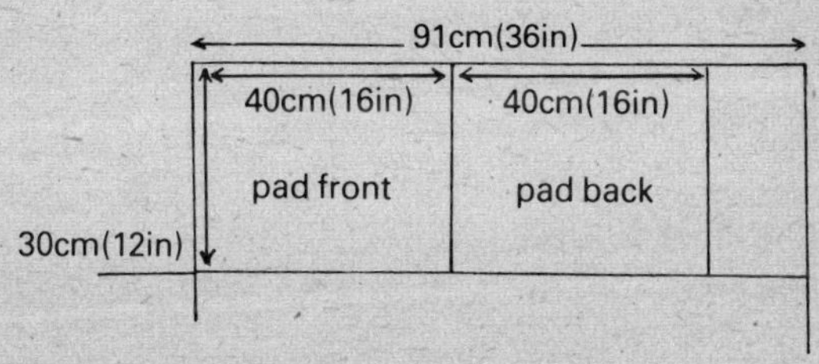

Figure 39   Cutting plan for a pillow cushion

Cut the fabric as on the cutting plan for pad and cover. Seam up the pad with 13 mm ($\frac{1}{2}$ in) turnings and fill (*as above*).

Cover

1.   Prepare crossway strips, joining, enclosing the cord and tacking (*see* Chapter 5).
2.   Set the cord round the edge of the cover top, matching raw edges and clipping piping casing to turn the corners. Join casing and cord.
3.   Machine the piping in place.
4.   Prepare the Velcro strips and insert at this stage (*see* Chapter 6).
5.   Machine the top and bottom of the cushion together using first machine line as a guide.
6.   Trim and neaten the seams with overcasting by hand or with machine zig-zag (*see* Chapter 3).

Alternative fastenings

Strap and facing or side zip   Follow stages 1, 2 and 3 above, then refer to instructions for chosen fastening in Chapter 6.

2.   A piped bordered cushion

35 cm (14 in) square with a 7.5 cm (3 in) border, filled with foam crumbs. Made in plain fabric with a zip centred on one border.

Materials

Cover	Pad
70 cm ($\frac{3}{4}$ yd) of 120 cm (48 in) fabric	60 cm ($\frac{2}{3}$ yd) of 91 cm (36 in) fabric
30 cm (12 in) zip	Approx $1\frac{1}{2}$ lb foam crumbs
260 cm (3 yd) piping cord	Sewing thread

Pad

Cut as cutting plan.

1.   Join border strips together leaving 13 mm ($\frac{1}{2}$ in) unstitched each end of the seam and checking the length of the strips.
2.   Place RS border to one square section RS, matching and turning the corners at seam points (Fig. 41a).
3.   Repeat on the other square section, leaving an opening for filling.
4.   Fill and stitch up.

Cutting plan   (Fig. 40)

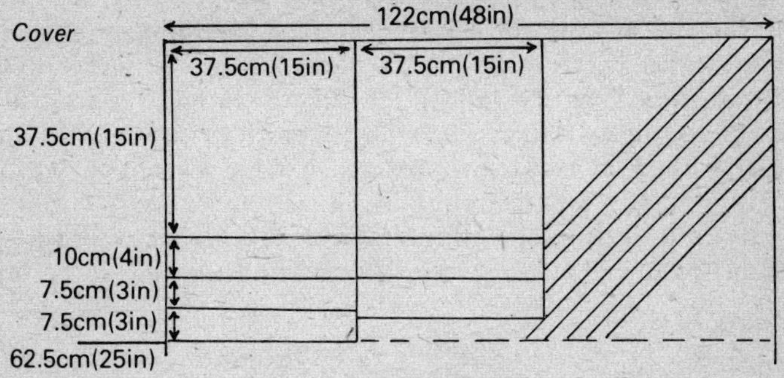

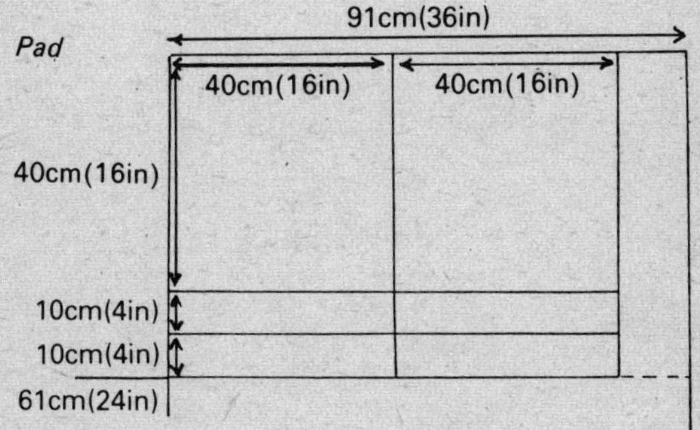

Figure 40   Cutting plan for a piped, bordered cushion

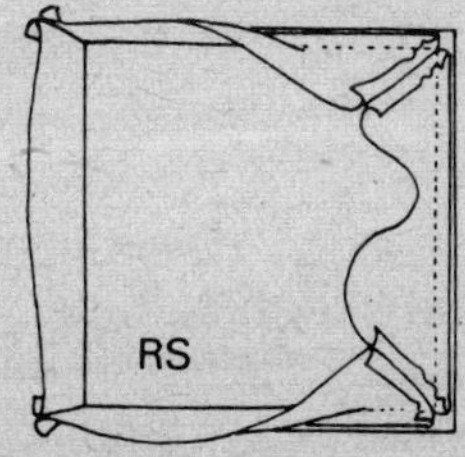

Figure 41a

Cover
1.   Follow instructions for a centre zip (*see* Chapter 6) between two narrower border strips (1 in – 2.5 cm turning allowed) and then match against the remaining 10 cm (4 in) strips, trimming if necessary.
2.   Make up the border strips as for the pad.
3.   Prepare the piping and apply it round both raw edges of the border strip. Clip the piping casing at corner seam points (Fig. 41b).
4.   Pin, tack and machine one square section of the cover to border strip similarly as for pad, matching and turning the corners neatly.
5.   Pin, tack and machine the other section of the cover to the border strip (remembering to undo the zip first). Neaten piped raw edges (Fig. 41c).

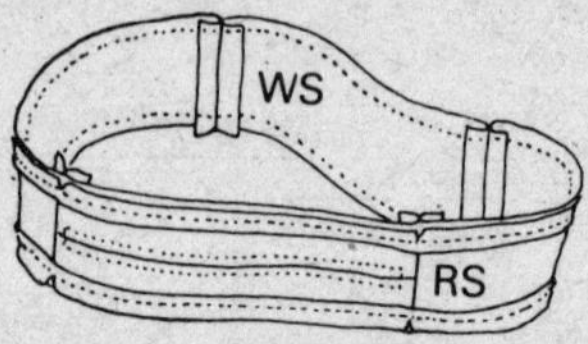

Figure 41b

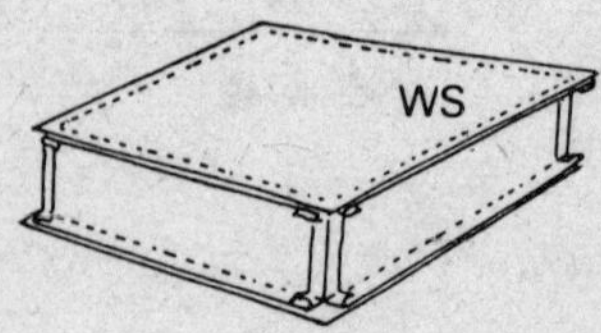

Figure 41c

Variations on this cushion
1.   It is not always necessary for the border to have a seam at each corner although this does help the cushion to keep in shape. An alternative is a continuous strip round, but as this will need joining somewhere, make sure the joins are placed symmetrically and inconspicuously.
2.   If the cushion is to have a firm or rigid filling (e.g. spring unit) an opening down one side will be insufficient and the opening must be taken round the corners.

3.   A circular cushion is better made with a border to accommodate the filling, rather than as a simple pillow cushion. Padding a flat article will always draw the outer edges inwards and in the case of a circle this means the distance round the circumference will be reduced causing the edge to develop an unattractive 'frilling'. By providing depth for the filling with a border this is prevented and the edges retain their smooth curve.

4.   If a centre back fastening is not suited to a particular bordered cushion which still needs to be used either way up this presents problems. Setting a fastening into a seam between the top and a border involves setting it into an angle and also possibly into a curve as well. The most suitable fastening is a strap and facing, or possibly reinforcing the opening edge with tape and sewing it up (*see Note* below).

Note: In the making-up instructions above the piping was applied to the border rather than to the square top section as it is easier to follow the first machine line and watch the corners with the border strip uppermost when working the second line of stitching. However this is only possible when the fastening is centred on a border; if it is set to the side of a border it must be concealed by the piping and therefore the piping must be set to one of the main sections first.

3.   Bolster cushion

A bolster cushion is really a circular bordered cushion with a very deep border. Often the circular ends are gathered into a central button or tassel and piped to give a firm outline.

To calculate the length of the straight central portion needed to fit the circular ends, the mathematical formula based on pi is used (the circumference of a circle is equal to its diameter (or twice its radius) multiplied by pi ($\frac{22}{7}$ or 3·174)).

To make a cushion 35 cm (14 in) wide with 18 cm (7 in) diameter with gathered circular ends

Calculating the measurements

The circumference of 7 in circle will be $\frac{22}{7} \times 7 = 22$ in or the circumference of 18 cm circle will be $18 \times 3 \cdot 174 = 57$ cm. Therefore the finished size of the centre rectangle must be

$$35 \text{ cm} \times 57 \text{ cm or } 14 \text{ in} \times 22 \text{ in}$$

The gathered ends will also have this same circumference measurement and as they gather in to a central button will need to be as wide as the radius (plus turnings).

It is usual to mount the gathered ends on to circles of calico before attaching them to the tubular section.

Fig. 42 shows the various sections of the bolster cushion (*Note:* Pins drawn larger for clarity).

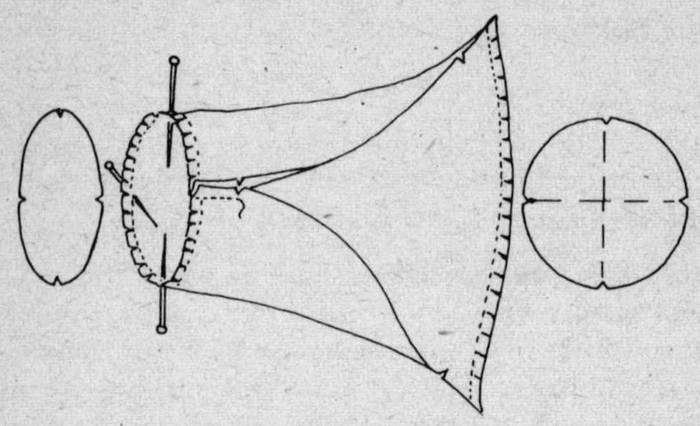

Figure 42a   Bolster cushion pad

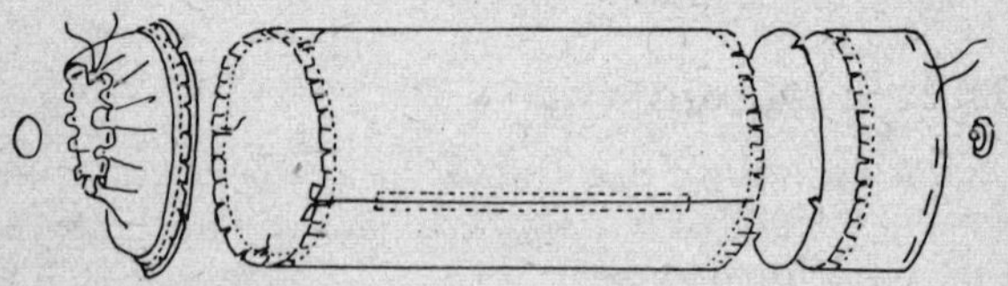

Figure 42b   Bolster cushion cover

The neatest way of fastening a bolster cushion is with a zip set into the seam of the 'tube'.

Cutting plan for a bolster cushion using striped fabric   (Fig. 43)
($\frac{3}{4}$ in – 2 cm turnings have been allowed on all seams)

Materials

Cover
60 cm ($\frac{2}{3}$ yd of 122 cm (48 in) fabric
30cm (12 in) zip
120 cm ($1\frac{1}{2}$ yd) piping cord

Pad
50 cm ($\frac{1}{2}$ yd) of 122 cm (48 in) lining fabric
(sufficient for 2 extra circles as foundation for top cover ends)

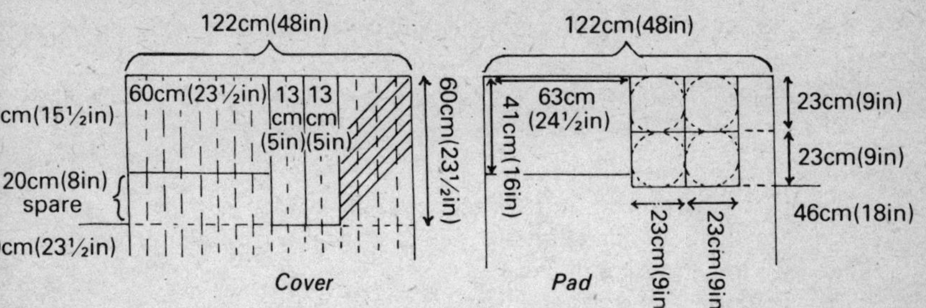

Figure 43   Cutting plan using striped fabric

Pad   (Refer to Fig. 42a)

1.   On the rectangular piece of lining fabric machine a line of stay-stitching down the seam line of the 63 cm (24½ in) edges and clip into these at 2 cm (¾ in) intervals.

2.   Bring the 41 cm (16 in) edges together, WS out, and seam them up leaving a gap in the centre for inserting the filling and leaving 2 cm (¾ in) or the amount of seam allowance unstitched each end of the seam.

3.   Mark quarter points round each stay-stitched end of the 'tube' and quarter end circles similarly.

4.   Matching the quarter marks, pin, tack and machine 'tube' section to end circles. Fill the pad and sew up the opening.

Cover   (Refer to Fig. 42b)

Assemble the rectangular central 'tube' similarly to pad, leaving an opening in the seam for the zip. Insert central zip (*see* Chapter 6).

Preparation of end circles

1.   Machine a line of stay-stitching down one long side of each strip 2 cm (¾ in) from the raw edge.

2.   Join the short edges of each strip to form two 'tubes' and press the seams flat.

3.   Divide the stay-stitched edges into quarters, similarly to main section.

4.   Along the other raw edge run a line of gathers, using strong thread and big stitches (about 2.5 cm (1 in) apart) – don't draw up the gathers yet.

5.   Quarter-mark the foundation circles and match these to the stay-stitched edges of the two small 'tubes', WS together. Tack in place round the stay-stitching line.

6.   Draw up the central gathers, at the same time arranging them evenly and pushing the raw edges down through the centre.

7.   Fasten off the gathering threads and cover the centre with a button or tassel.
8.   Prepare the piping and machine it round the edge of the circles along the stay-stitching line.

Assembling cushion cover
1.   Undo the zip and turn the main section to WS.
2.   Matching the quarter marks, pin, tack and sew the main section to the end circles, enclosing piping.
3.   Trim the raw edges and neaten.

4.   Neck cushion

These are very easy to make and only two points must be observed:

1.   Make sure that the top angle of the pattern is a right-angle, otherwise the cushion develops an unsightly point each end.
2.   It is easiest to assemble the four sections in pairs first and then to bring together and seam all round.

Pattern
Cut *four pieces* as diagram (Fig. 44) making the length about 18 in – 45 cm.

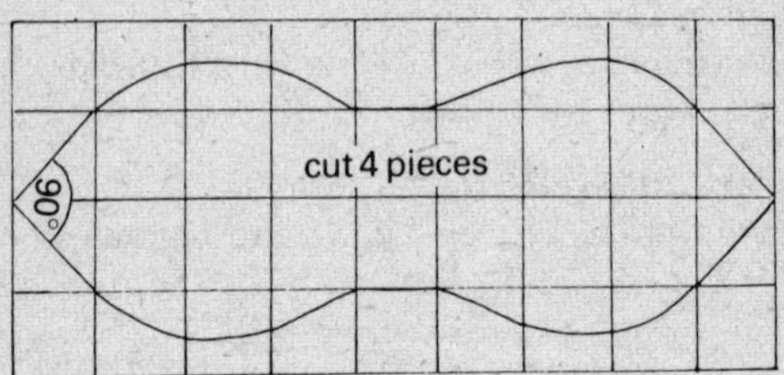

Figure 44   Pattern for a neck cushion

Note: It is possible to insert a central zip down one seam before assembling, but the curve of the pattern makes it difficult to keep flat. Perhaps one of the most popular versions of this cushion is that made from towelling filled with foam which, being washable, can be sewn up.

13 Curtains (drapes)

Curtain planning

The whole appearance of a window – or even a whole room – can be altered by the type of curtains chosen. Both the day and night-time affect of the curtains must be considered i.e. when they are drawn back from the window, as well as when they are drawn across.

Fig. 45 shows how a simple pair of windows can be made to appear quite different by variations in the fittings, grouping and length of the curtains.

Figure 45

When deciding what type of curtains to have, consider the *function* of the particular curtains planned. Are they:

1.   for decorative appearance only, from inside or outside;
2.   for insulation from cold, the sun, or noise;
3.   for privacy;
4.   to obscure an ugly view;
5.   to improve the proportions of the window or room.

Again, will they need to be lined or unlined? Some reasons for choosing *unlined* curtains could be:

1.   they are cheap;
2.   they are easy to launder;
3.   the window is too small to take the added bulk of a lining;
4.   the fabric you have chosen is reversible;
5.   there is no need for insulation;
6.   you want to give a light 'filmy' look to a window.

Some reasons for choosing lined curtains could be:
1.   the need for insulation;
2.   the fabric chosen is not washable (e.g. velvet);
3.   the fabric chosen is unattractive on wrong side;
4.   wanting all curtains to look alike from outside;
5.   wanting curtains to give a 'rich' appearance.

Detachable lining

This is in a way a compromise between lined and unlined curtains. It is a lining headed with a special tape which encloses the top raw edge and provides a series of small holes through which the hooks supporting the main curtain can pass. It enables curtain and lining to be cleaned separately, and for the lining to be removed, say, in summer, and put back in winter. The fact that the curtain and lining are made separately means that the curtain, when making up, is treated as unlined. It is a good plan to stitch press-studs or Velcro on in a few places to hold curtain and lining together.

Fittings

Developments in the range are occuring all the time, but they fall broadly into four categories:

1.   Expanded wire
One of the oldest, cheapest and simplest types of fittings, and still popular

today for light-weight curtains that do not need drawing. Usually sold with a plastic coating, they are fixed under tension to a hook and eyelet either end. The disadvantages are that they tend to sag in the middle and they are not ideal for draw curtains. It is usual to make curtains for this type of fitting with a heading through which the wire is threaded, but occasionally split rings are used. They are used for glass curtains, small curtains across cupboards etc.

2.   Simple rods, dowelling etc.

People are apt to forget that these make a very satisfactory and cheap curtain fitting in the right setting. Dowelling can be painted, stained and varnished, and fitted to a window or wall with cup-hooks. Again, curtains may be made either with a heading or with commercial tape and rings.

3.   Curtain tracks

These have been developed and improved a great deal in recent years, being made in plastic as well as the original metal. Improved methods of fixing the rod to the wall for easy removal have been invented, and a variety of ways have been evolved for the runners to travel along the track; some being a combined hook and runner, some being recessed so that the track itself is almost invisible, whilst others make a feature of a decorative track with ornamental ends (finials). Combined with many of these are cording systems. Points to help in selection are:

(*a*) If a pelmet or valance is planned, the appearance of the track won't matter. Some suppliers make a combined track and valance rail.
(*b*) Consider the *weight* of curtaining. A more robust track may be needed with special smooth-running fittings and a cording system if heavy inter-lined curtains are planned.
(*c*) Not all tracks will bend round bay windows. Check this.
(*d*) If you are planning curtains to hang directly beneath the track it is better not to choose a type combining hook and runner as the hooks will be visible above the curtain.

4.   Decorative rods and poles

These come in all types, colours, sizes and materials, with or without decorative fixings and finials, and cording systems. Moreover, not all are round in section, but some are shaped like a 'D' with rounded face and flattened back, taking a D-shaped curtain ring. Most rod-rings have a small eyelet at the base into which the curtain is hooked, mounted on commercial heading tape, so that the curtain hangs beneath the rod.

Blinds
These should not be overlooked, as there are occasions when they are more suitable than curtains, or can be combined with curtains to create a special effect. The advantages of blinds, besides their obvious decorative appeal, are that:

1.   they need no room for draw-back, letting in maximum light, so are often the solution for difficult windows such as dormer-windows;
2.   they are neatly out of the way when not in use, making them ideal for rooms such as kitchens when curtains would get dirty quickly.

Unfortunately, room does not permit here for going into detail on different styles of blinds, of which there are many, but besides the ready-made roller-type blinds, there are a number of blind-making kits on the market, available at stores and through mail-order, all of which supply clear easy-to-follow instructions.

Curtain headings
Commercial tapes are available for all kinds of headings. The most familiar are tapes woven with a pocket to take a hook – the tape sometimes reinforced for added stiffness – and with draw-cords forming gathers or pleats. Some are made with pockets only to take multi-legged hooks to form pleats. With this range of tapes, simple gathered, pencil, cartridge and pinch pleats and decorative shirred (multi-gathered) headings can be produced. A less common combined heading reinforcement and pleating strip is available; this consists of a plastic strip marked into 'scored' pleating divisions which is inserted into the heading and stitched in place.

Special heading buckram is also available for stiffening curtain headings.

Varieties of commercial tape to look for are:

1.   Tape made of special light-weight fibres for sheer fabrics, e.g. 'Tervoil'.
2.   Tape with reinforcing nylon threads for extra support.
3.   Tape woven with pockets to take hooks at a variety of levels on the tape. For pinch pleats some tapes are made specially to suit the hanging position, e.g. 'Underslung'.
4.   Tapes with cords designed to draw up the heading decoratively in various multi-gathered effects. These usually involve stitching the tape centrally as well as at top and bottom, when stitching it to the curtain.

When considering the question of stiffening the heading it is worth bearing in mind that, unless the heading has to stand up above the hooks, this is not generally necessary, although pinch pleats can look crisper if interlined.

Net (glass) curtain headings
The most usual way to buy glass curtains nowadays is in the form of ready-headed and hemmed lengths, purchasing to the nearest 'drop' the yardage, or metreage needed to give the required fullness across the window (sometimes called brise-bise). Because one is purchasing to a set 'drop' it is often necessary to alter the heading to exactly fit the window length and this can be easily done by unpicking the chain-stitching and re-stitching another simple double heading.

If you are making cross-over net curtains, overlap and tack the top edges before forming the heading, then handle the double thickness as one heading.

Measuring for curtains

1. Length   (Fig. 46)
Difficulty is often experienced in deciding from which point to take an accurate lengthwise measurement. Professional curtain-makers usually take the length from the 'hook drop', which is the small eye in the runner through which the hook passes. However this does not give all the information needed for cutting out and making up without knowing whether the heading is to rise above the track or hang beneath. It is easier to visualise the finished curtain hanging from the rail and take a measurement from where the top of the curtain is to come in relation to the rail down to the bottom of the curtain – to the sill, below the sill or just clear of the ground. This will be the actual measurement of the finished curtain with the hem turned up and the heading turned down. Positioning the heading tape so that the hooks will line up with the runners can be checked when attaching the tape finally.

2. Width
This must be taken from the actual length of the curtain track which may be within the window recess or extend each side outside the recess to give room for drawing back the curtains. Some rails also provide for curtains to overlap in the middle, and this must also be borne in mind.

Additions to length and width measurements
To the *length* measurement must be added:
A *hem allowance* which is folded *double* and may vary in depth from 5 cm to 10 cm (2 in to 4 in) depending on:

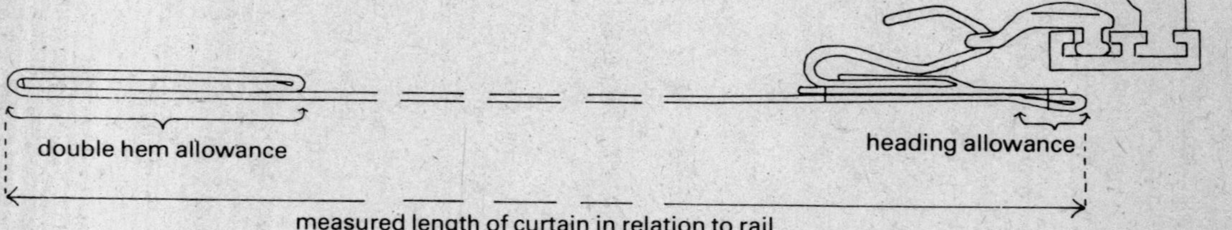

Figure 46   Measuring for curtains

(*a*) the proportions of the curtain;
(*b*) the amount of spare fabric if cutting to a pattern repeat;
(*c*) the weight of the fabric.

Initially allow at least 10 cm (4 in)

A *heading allowance* must also be added which will depend on the type of heading and tape and its position on the rail. If you are using a deep tape as little as 13 mm ($\frac{1}{2}$ in) may be allowed as most of these tapes are stitched to the top folded edge of the curtain, but if using a standard gathering tape, it is usual to allow for a frill above the tape (unless covered by a pelmet or valance) and in this case add 5 cm – 7·5 cm (2 in – 3 in).

To the *width* measurement must be added an allowance for:
(*a*) side hems of 4 cm (1$\frac{1}{2}$ in) on each curtain;
(*b*) any fabric joins across the curtain width;
(*c*) fullness, depending on the type of heading (*see* Chapter 9).

Note: Don't forget, when planning fullness, to bear in mind the amount of space available for drawing back curtains.

To calculate total metrage (yardage) needed

The *length* measurement plus allowances will give the total metrage (yardage) for *1 width* of curtaining.

The *width* measurement plus allowances will tell you *how many widths* of fabric are needed across the window, calculating to the nearest width (or, occasionally, half-width).

When calculating for a *pattern match* (which must match right across a window from curtain to curtain) this is done by calculating the nearest multiple of pattern repeats after the first cut length. For example, if the pattern repeats every 30 cm (12 in) and the cut curtain requires three lengths of 170 cm (68 in), the amount of fabric will be 170 cm (68 in) plus two lengths of 180 cm (72 in) (180 cm (72 in) being the nearest multiple of 30 cm (12 in)), making a total fabric requirement of 5.30 m (5 yd 2 ft 8 in or 6 yd). It is sometimes even safer to buy entirely to the pattern repeat, i.e. three times 180 cm (72 in) as this gives greater freedom for positioning the pattern motif.

Fig. 47 shows a simple window with a track measuring 122 cm (4 ft) for which it is planned to make pencil-pleated curtains hanging beneath the track to a length of 100 cm (39$\frac{1}{2}$ in).

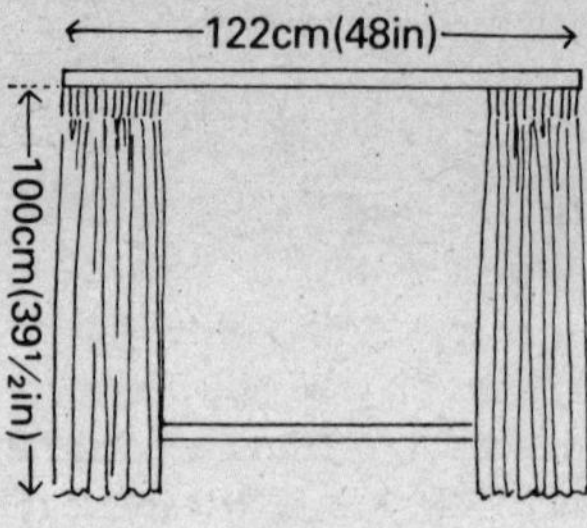

Figure 47

To calculate fabric requirement

Length

$$100 \text{ cm} + 10\text{cm (hem)} + 2 \cdot 5 \text{ cm (heading)} = 112 \cdot 5 \text{ cm}$$
$$(39\tfrac{1}{2} \text{ in} + \quad 4 \text{ in} \qquad + 1 \text{ in} \qquad\qquad = 44\tfrac{1}{2} \text{ in})$$

Width

Track length	122 cm	(48 in)
Fullness for pencil pleats	224 cm	(96 in)
4 side-hems of 4 cm (1½ in)	16 cm	(6 in)
2 joins (1½ widths to each curtain)	5 cm	(2 in)
	387 cm	(152 in)

Needing 3 fabric widths of 122 cm (48 in) to give 366 cm (144 in), therefore 3 × 112·5 cm (44½ in) = 337·5 cm (133½ in) and total metrage (yardage) needed will be 3·40 m (3¾ yd) for *plain fabric*.

Note: The width of 366 cm is, or course, less than the calculated width of 387 cm. This does not matter, as it is near enough, and the difference will be accommodated in the pleats. It would not make sense to buy a further width of material.

For fabric with a *51 cm (20 in) pattern repeat* the requirement would be:

(*a*) First cut length 112·5 cm (44½in).
(*b*) Nearest pattern repeat multiple is (3) 153 cm (60 in).
(*c*) Two lengths of this multiple are 306 cm (120 in).

Therefore the fabric needed will be:

$$112 \cdot 5 \text{ cm} + 306 \text{ cm} = 418 \cdot 5 \text{ cm}$$
$$(44\tfrac{1}{2} \text{ in}) + (120 \text{ in}) = (164\tfrac{1}{2} \text{ in})$$

Lining is cut to the measured length of the curtain less 2·5 cm (1 in) to which is added:
(*a*) a heading allowance the same as for the curtain;
(*b*) a hem allowance (double) usually 2·5 cm (1 in) narrower than the curtain hem.

Selvedges

The strengthening threads that make up the selvedge are apt to draw up the fabric at the edges, and spoil the hang of the curtain. To prevent this, either cut them off completely, or clip into them at intervals of about 10 cm (4 in).

Making curtains

(i) Unlined   (Fig. 48)

1.   *Cutting out*   Curtains should always be cut square to the selvedge or warp, i.e. with corners at right angles. This is easiest to do on a square-edged table, lining up the sides of fabric and table so that the position of the cut rests on the table edge and the chalk can be run along the table edge. Times when this cannot be done are:

(*a*) when there is a *very* obvious grain, e.g. a woven stripe, which must be followed.
(*b*) when the pattern repeat across the fabric is not square (*see* Chapter 2) in which case the pattern must be followed.

Carefully mark with chalk the lengths to be cut down the fabric, chalk in the cutting line as above, and cut cleanly across. (Check pattern matches carefully – *see* Chapter 2.)
2.   Make any joins across the fabric width with a *rolled seam* (*see* Chapter 3) matching pattern if necessary and slip-tacking (*see* Chapter 3).
3.   Using a *template* (*see* Chapter 2) fold down and tack a 1 cm – 2·5 cm ($\frac{1}{2}$ in – 1 in) double hem down each side. Slip-hem in place using a *weight*, or stitch by machine.
4.   Turn up the lower hem (using a *template*) to form a double hem of depth allowed for and slip-hem (*see* Chapter 3, Fig. 6) in place, using the *weight*. Corners need not be mitred but the hem may be tapered in slightly to prevent the edge from showing.
5.   *Squaring up*   This is an important part of the curtain-making process ensuring that the curtain hem hangs level. Lay the curtain, face up, on a flat surface, and with a firm ruler measure up about every 15 cm (6 in) from the hem for the total finished length (your original measurement) inserting

a pin each time to mark the top of the heading. Ensure the ruler is straight.
6.   Turn the curtain over to the WS and fold down the heading along the pin line. Tack along the folded edge *either* 6 mm ($\frac{1}{4}$ in) from the folded edge, if attaching deep heading tape, *or* at the depth of the top frill if using standard tape, thus giving a guide line for positioning the tape.

Figure 48   Unlined curtain

7.   *Attaching tape*   Withdraw sufficient cord from one end to enable a knot to be tied. Tuck under with the raw edge of the tape and tack the tape in position along the heading under slight tension. Leave the cord ends free at the other end of the tape, just turning under raw edge. Machine the tape in place.

(ii) Lined curtains   (Fig. 49)

Cut fabric and lining carefully (*see* cutting instructions for unlined curtains) and make any joins across the width with a flat seam (*see* Chapter 3).

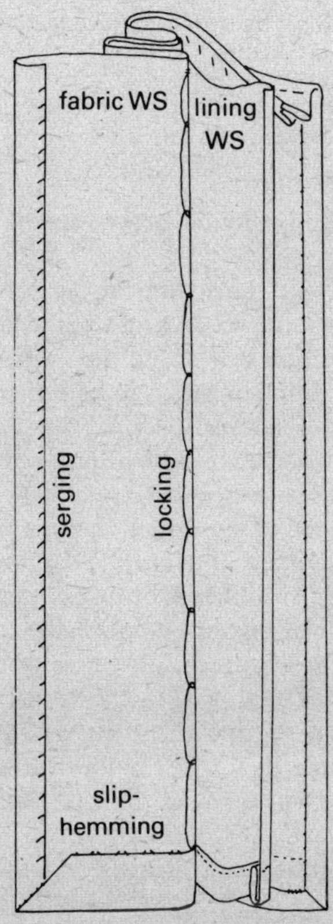

Figure 49   *Lined curtain*

Fabric

1. Using a *template* fold down a single hem down each side of the curtain. The average width of a side hem is 4 cm (1½ in) but if using a patterned fabric with a wide margin, run a 2·5 cm (1 in) *template* down the patterned edge to ensure only the pattern is visible when the lining is attached (*see* Chapter 1).

2. Using a *template* fold up a double hem along the lower edge to the depth allowed. Press the hem.

3. Turn back the fabric at the lower corners and refold it to form a hem *mitre* (*see* Chapter 10). Press.

4. Pin and tack turnings and mitres in place.

5. Serge stitch side hems, slip-stitch mitre edges together and slip-hem lower hem (*see* Chapter 3).

Lining

6. Using a *template*, press a double hem along the lower edge. Machine in place.

7. Smooth curtain, WS up, on a large flat surface and place the lining, RS up over it so that the top raw edges match, the lower hem of the lining leaves a 2·5 cm (1 in) margin below, and the sides are evenly positioned. Pin hems of fabric and lining together, to hold them in position.

8. *Locking* This is worked vertically: it is usual to lock any seams together and make a further two locking joins per curtain width, i.e. a single width curtain will have two locking joins between the side hems. Commence near the centre of the curtain, unpinning along the hem first on one side and then the other, in order to fold back the lining to the locking position (*see* Chapter 3). As a line of locking is worked, re-pin the hem. Lines of locking should run from the top raw edge to the top of the hems, but if the heading is to be interlined, leave at least 10 cm (4 in) unlocked so that the interlining can be slipped in after squaring up.

9. Turn the side edges of the lining in to leave a 2·5 cm (1 in) margin and slip-stitch in place. (If interlining the heading, leave the top 10 cm (4 in) unstitched.) Take the stitching round the lower corner of the lining for about 2.5 cm (1 in).

10. If not inserting an interlining, diagonal tack the curtain to the lining along the heading edge.

11. *Squaring up See* instructions for the unlined curtain (5).

12. If not interlining the heading, turn down and attach the tape as for an unlined curtain (6 and 7).

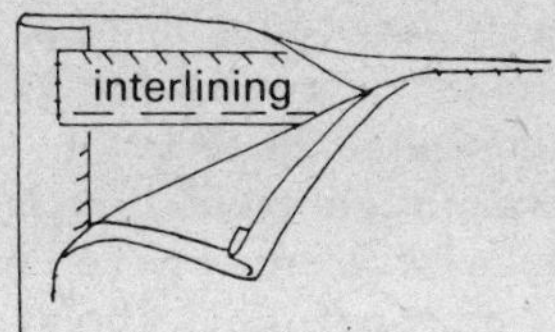

Figure 50a   Hand-pleated interlining heading

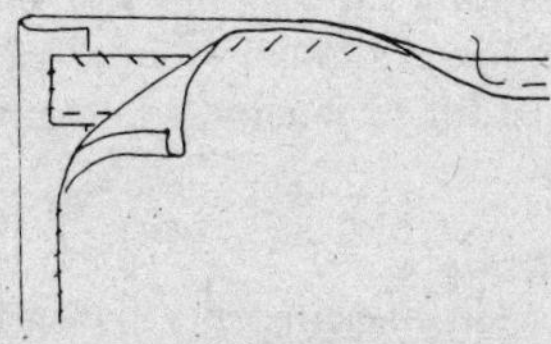

Figure 50b   Interlined heading using commercial tape

13.   *Interlined heading*   (Fig. 50).

(*a*) *Hand-made pinch pleats*   Fold back lining and place top edge of inter-lining to pin-marked fold postition lightly catching in place with serge-stitching. Tack the lower edge of the interlining to the curtain. Fold the top of the raw edge down over the interlining along the fold line and serge-stitch to interlining. Bring the lining back over the interlining, turn the top edge under so that it can be hemmed in place just short of the fold line.

(*b*) *With heading tape*   Insert interlining between the curtain fabric and the lining, matching the top edge to the pinned fold-line, and tack in place. Tack the raw edges of lining and curtain together, then turn down the heading and attach the tape as for the unlined curtain.

14.   Remove the tacking and finish slip-stitching up the sides of the lining.

Added insulation

This can be provided in two ways, by milium or bump.

Milium   This is a lining fabric coated on one side (the inner side) with fine aluminium particles. It provides effective heat insulation in winter and protection from the sun in summer. It is dearer than standard curtain lining, but is handled in exactly the same way, being available in a range of shades 122 cm (48 in) wide. It has to be dry-cleaned, not washed, but could be hung from a separate lining tape if used in conjunction with washable curtain fabric.

Bump   (*see* Chapter 7)   This is an interlining, placed between curtain fabric and lining. It is cheaper than Milium but, of course, is not a substitute for a lining, so may not work out much cheaper. It involves additional work in making up, as it needs to be locked to the curtain, similarly to a lining; additional locking is also necessary along the hem fold lines. It is cut to the same size as the curtain fabric and, after locking, bump and fabric are handled together, as one fabric. This interlining provides excellent insulation, giving curtains a heavy appearance which can make the fabric look richer. However, because of this bulk, care should be taken to check that there is sufficient room for drawing back, and sufficient drop to produce a good drape. Although bump, by itself, is washable, it is inclined to shrink and alter dimensionally, so should not be washed in the curtain.

Curtain hooks and rings

These are available in various designs and materials the majority being designed for sliding into specially woven pockets on commercial tape. Multi-pronged hooks are sold for special pleating tapes. It is possible to buy hooks with a pin end for inserting into headings where a tape is not used. Alternatively there are hooks available for sewing on by hand (using strong thread and buttonhole stitch).

If using a commercial gathering tape, space out and insert hooks before drawing up the heading (every 10 cm (4 in)).

Drawing up the curtain

It improves the appearance of the gathers if the tape is drawn up as tightly as it will go and then released back to the correct width. Always allow a little more than the actual length of the curtain fitting when drawing up. In the case of the stiffer tapes, such as Spantape, tie the cord ends to something rigid like a door handle and pull against it to draw up the gathers.

The spare cord, after drawing up, may be wound on a cord tidy (made by manufacturers of curtain hooks and fittings) or be wound round the fingers in a figure-of-eight and lightly stitched to an inconspicuous place near the heading tape.

14 Pelmets

A pelmet is a smooth stiffened strip of fabric concealing the curtain track.
It is usually attached to a pelmet board and gives a decorative but formal
trim to the top of a window. The traditional stiffening for a pelmet is
buckram containing size which is used during the making-up process. A
narrow width, sold specially for pelmets, can often be bought from furnishing stores; this enables a pelmet to be cut economically without needing
joins which are apt to show. Alternatively modern interlinings are now
available, such as heavy Vilene, but need different handling as they do not
contain size.

Planning

The average proportional depth of a pelmet in relation to the curtain depth
should be *one-twelfth* at its narrowest part. This can, however, depend on
the amount of decorative shaping and its total length. Often, on a straight
pelmet with little decoration, one-ninth gives a better effect. If in doubt,
draw a template in paper and try it in situ.

Measuring

The length of a pelmet is taken along the pelmet board, taking in the front
edge, the sides (return) and, if there is room between wall and board, an
additional 2·5 cm (1 in) round the back edge of the board (false return)
which helps to hold the side edges in a 'boxed' position.

Method of fixing

In the past it was usual to place a tack tape behind the top edge, stitching
it to form a series of 'pockets', through which drawing pins or tacks were
inserted to fix pelmet to board. A far simpler and more convenient method
nowadays is to use Velcro, stitching the 'velvety' side to the back edge of
the pelmet, and nailing with tacks or stapling toothed (or hooked) section to
the outside edge of the board.

To make a pelmet

Materials

1. Besides fabric and buckram, a strip of bump is required to insert between buckram and fabric.

2. *Lining* fabric is used to neaten the back, hiding the buckram.

3. *Gimp* or *braid* is usually stitched to the lower edge of the pelmet, defining the shape.

4. *Velcro* (or 4 cm (1½ in) tack tape) will be needed for the length of the pelmet board (including return and false return).

Cutting out

1. *Cut* the buckram and bump to size and shape required for finished pelmet.

2. Cut the fabric to the same shape *adding* 2·5 cm (1 in) to the sides and lower edge, and 4 cm (1½ in) to the top edge.

3. Cut the lining to shape, *adding* 13 mm (½ in) to the sides and lower edge only.

Avoid, if possible, making joins in buckram, but it may be necessary to join fabric and bump. Edges of bump should be butted (placed edge to edge) and oversewn, not seamed or overlapped or a ridge will show. The fabric should have the pattern carefully centred and matched, paying attention to design in relation to the shaping on the pelmet edge.

Making-up   (Fig. 51)

The hardest part of making a pelmet is the handling of the buckram which, because of its stiffness, cannot be 'picked up' in the needle but needs to be stabbed through. The problem is minimised if the following method is followed:

1. Match edges of bump and buckram and stitch together all round using big stitches. (Strong thread and a heavy needle are needed – a leather needle works well.) Work sitting at a table and hold the buckram just off the edge so that the needle can be stabbed up and down. Trim bump edges level with the buckram (Fig. 51a).

2. On fabric WS rule a chalk line on the grain to indicate the 4 cm (1½ in) turning allowance along the top edge. Lap the top edge of the buckram, bump side up, to meet the chalk mark, and pin in place. Fold the fabric over buckram edge to RS and bring the two boxed sides of the pelmet into their finished positions to check that the face fabric does not strain and distort the buckram. Adjust pins if necessary (Fig. 51b).

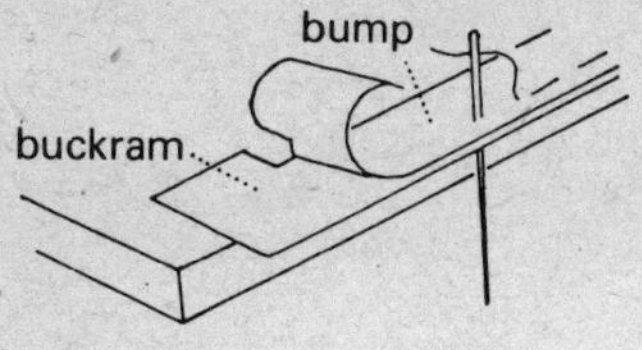

Figure 51a

Figure 51b

3.   Place pelmet flat on the table once more but this time have fabric RS uppermost and towards you whilst the buckrum (bump side down) rests on the edge of the table. Tack the fabric to the buckram about 2 cm ($\frac{3}{4}$ in) from the edge of the buckram (Fig. 51c).

4.   Position 'velvety' (looped) section of Velcro over tacking so that it comes just short of the top edge of the buckram, and stitch in place (stab-stitches about 1 cm ($\frac{3}{8}$ in) apart) along both edges leaving *unstitched* the last 2·5 cm (1 in) each end to enable the fabric corners to be mitred (Fig. 51d).

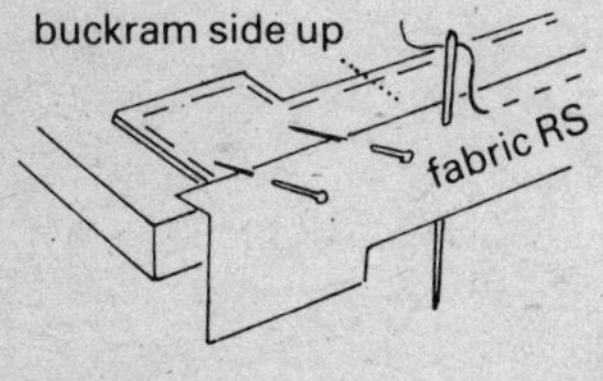

Figure 51c

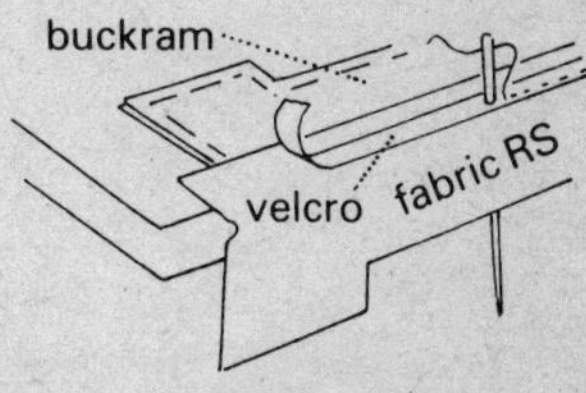

Figure 51d

Note: If using *tack tape,* position as Velcro, stab-stitching in place along the lower edge and again 2·5 cm (1 in) above; then catch down the free top 15 mm ($\frac{1}{2}$ in) at 10 cm (4 in) intervals to form pockets for the tacks.

5.   Turn the pelmet over and smooth the fabric down over the bump, ensuring that the grain is straight. Draw the lower edge to the side of the table and tack the fabric in place along the sides and lower edge. (Turnings are *not* folded under yet) (Fig. 51e). Keep tacking 1 cm ($\frac{3}{8}$ in) from the lower edge so it will be covered by trimming.

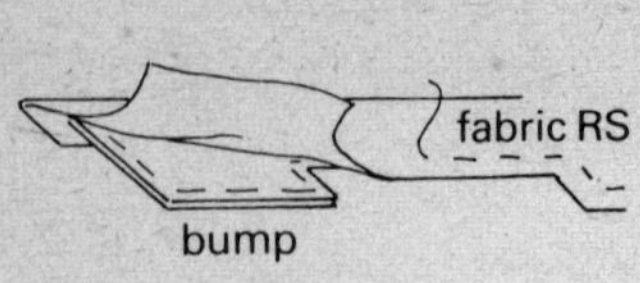

Figure 51e

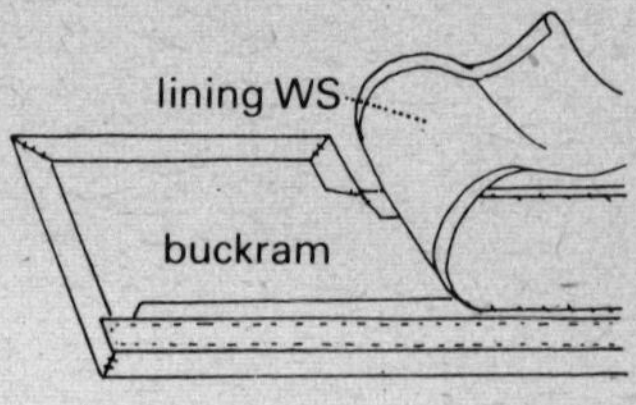

Figure 51f

6.   Turn the pelmet over to the buckram side and fold and press mitres (surplus fabric may be trimmed back). Clip the fabric carefully into angles where it needs to spread, overcasting any weak points.

7.   Damp the edges of the buckram to release the size and press the turnings down round the shaped edge and sides, sticking the fabric in place. Allow to cool and dry.

8.   Slip-stitch the mitres in place and stitch down the ends of the Velcro.

9.   Stab-stitch the braid, etc. along the lower edge.

10.   Slip-stitch lining in place on the back, following the line of the shaped edge and taking it up to the lower edge of the Velcro or tack tape. (It is easier to do this with a curved needle) (Fig. 51f).

15 Valances

A valance is a decorative frill which can be attached in various ways, depending on its purpose:

1.   stitched to supporting fabric, e.g. at the bottom of a loose cover;
2.   with press studs or Velcro, e.g. on a dressing table;
3.   with commercial heading tape to a valance rail;
4.   with a simple hemmed heading to expanded wire;
5.   with tacks (through tack tape) to a valance board, similarly to a pelmet.
   Depending on the method of attachment the heading for a valance can be formed of:

1.   gathering formed by commercial tape, or machine or hand stitching (*see* Chapter 3);
2.   the range of open-topped pleats formed by hand or with commerical tape – Pencil, Cartridge, French, Goblet, Pinch, Fluted, etc.;
3.   hand-pleating, suited to either setting in to, for example, the lower edge of a loose cover, or attaching to tape – box, box and space, knife or inverted pleats;
4.   occasional inverted pleats, for example at the corners of a loose cover valance (*see* Chapter 9).

Measuring for a valance
Depth
For a window, the proportion is usually one-ninth of the curtain depth or window.
Length
This measurement is taken along the fixing, i.e. the valance board or rail, or the distance round the chair or bed.
Allowances
As well as the fullness allowance in accordance with chosen gathers or pleats, provision must be made for:

(*a*) *if unlined*, a 2 cm ($\frac{3}{4}$ in) double hem at the bottom and sides (adding 4 cm ($1\frac{1}{2}$ in));

(*b*) *if lined*, a 2·5 cm (1 in) single hem at the bottom and sides; and
(*c*) *for either*, sufficient for heading or attaching, varying from 13 mm ($\frac{1}{2}$ in)
for a set-in valance, to 5 cm (2 in) for a gathered heading using heading tape.

To make

An *unlined valance* is made exactly like an unlined curtain.

A lined valance   (Fig. 52)
Cut the fabric to the size required and the lining 2·5 cm (1 in) shorter and
narrower than the fabric. Make any joins along the width with flat seams.

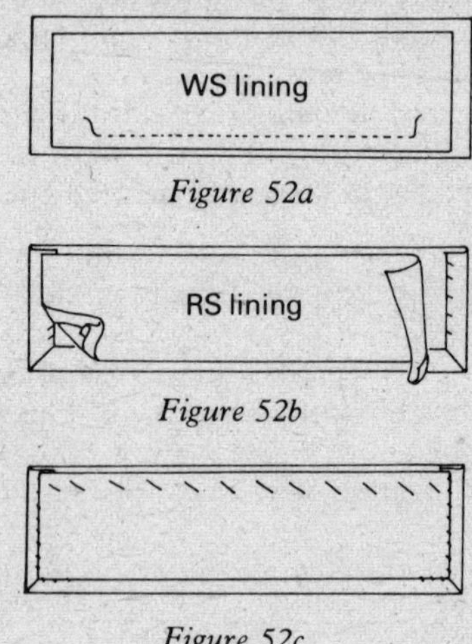

Figure 52a

Figure 52b

Figure 52c

1.   Place RS of lining to RS of fabric, adjusting the sides equally and
matching the lower raw edges. Machine the lower raw edges together with
a 13 mm ($\frac{1}{2}$ in) seam, leaving 5 cm (2 in) unstitched each end. Press the seam
towards the lining (Fig. 52a).
2.   Fold the fabric and lining RS out so that the top raw edges match and
a 12 mm ($\frac{1}{2}$ in margin of fabric shows at hem. Press.
3.   Fold the lining away from the sides, turn in side hems 2·5 cm (1 in) and
form corner mitres. Slip-stitch mitres and serge side hems (Fig. 52b).
4.   Turn under lining at sides to give a 13 mm ($\frac{1}{2}$ in) margin similar to the
hem and slip-stitch in place, including remainder of hem.
5.   Diagonal tack lining and fabric along the top edge (Fig. 52c).

Commercial tape   Attach as for the curtain.

Tack tape   (4 cm – 1½in):

1.   Fold the top edge of the valance down to the required depth and form pleats or gathers as required (*see* Chapter 9).
2.   Cut the tape to the size of the valance board plus 13 mm (½ in) at each end, and form this into a small hem to neaten the ends.
3.   Attach the tape to the valance with two lines of half-back stitch (*see* Chapter 3) worked from RS; one line worked along the bottom edge of the tape and the second line 2·5 cm (1 in) above, enclosing the raw edges of the heading.
4.   Form 'pockets' for the tacks along the top 13 mm (½ in) by stitching up to the top of the tape at 10 cm (4 in) intervals.

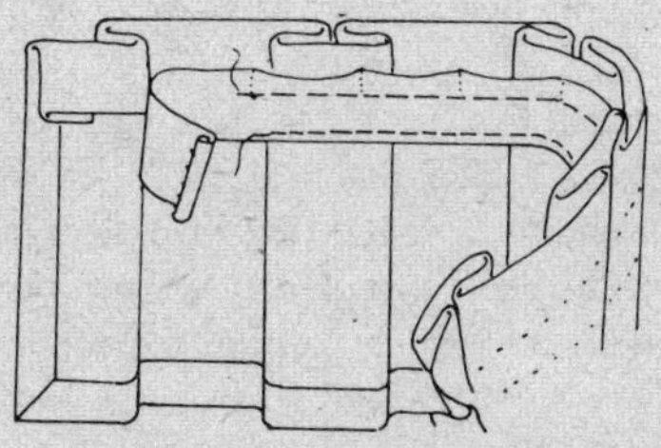

Figure 53   Applying tack tape

Velcro or *stud tape*   Cut length to the size of the valance board and sew to the back of the valance with half-back stitch, worked on RS, so that the turned down raw edge of the heading is enclosed between the stitching along the top and bottom edge of the tape or Velcro.

If *setting in* to supporting fabric, gather or pleat the raw edges of the prepared valance along the stitching line. Remember to mark centres, corners and/or quarter points to ensure even distribution of the fullness.

16 Simple loose covers (slip covers)

The term 'loose cover' does not mean a loose-fitting cover, but rather a cover that preserves the upholstery beneath and can be removed for cleaning.

Covers can be made to fit almost any shaped article, and it would be impossible in one short chapter to give adequate instructions for the making of all types. All that can be attempted here is to set out some of the basic principles whilst describing the making of a cover for a simple chair.

There are two principal finishes for loose covers: the tie-under and the valance. In the *tie-under* added material at the bottom of the cover is drawn underneath the chair where it is tied with tapes (*see* Chapter 5). This gives a smooth tailored finish. The *valance*, frill or flounce, is added to the lower edge of the cover, sometimes falling to floor level and hiding the legs of the chair.

As each style needs a different set of measurements, the finish must be decided before measuring the chair.

Measuring

The rule of 'thinking in rectangles' applies here, and measurements must be based on the widest parts in each direction. This is not as wasteful in fabric as it seems, and trying to cut paper patterns of a chair, or to cut a pattern from an old cover, is never very successful.

When taking loose cover measurements, it is important to note the *direction*, i.e. across (with weft) or down (with warp) and to get into the habit of keeping these measurements in separate columns when writing them down.

To the basic measurements must be *added*:

1.   A seam allowance of at least 13 mm ($\frac{1}{2}$ in), preferably more.
2.   At least another 13 cm (5 in) for a tie-under finish. (This amount would also be added for a tuck-in.)

Valance measurement: The *width* will be based on the distance round the chair, plus a fullness allowance for pleats or gathers. The *depth* of the valance must be decided in relation to the shape, style and proportions of the chair. For example, a small bedroom chair, depending on its style, could look attractive with either a short, or a floor level valance. The valance on an easy chair, whilst reaching to the floor, might look best at a depth of 15 cm (6 in) or 22·5 cm (9 in) depending on the chair's shape.

Piping: Remember to allow some fabric for this.

Estimating and cutting plan

If measurements have been kept in columns for width and length, it is fairly simple to run down the 'widths' column to see which pieces can be set side by side on the fabric width.

Pattern placement is important on loose covers so make sure that any obvious motif is centred and/or matched on each section that is prominently placed, for example, on a seat, or front border.

To make a loose cover for a simple chair

Figure 54 shows two styles of cover for the same chair, (a) with piped border and tie-under, (b) with darts and gathered valance; each will need different measurements.

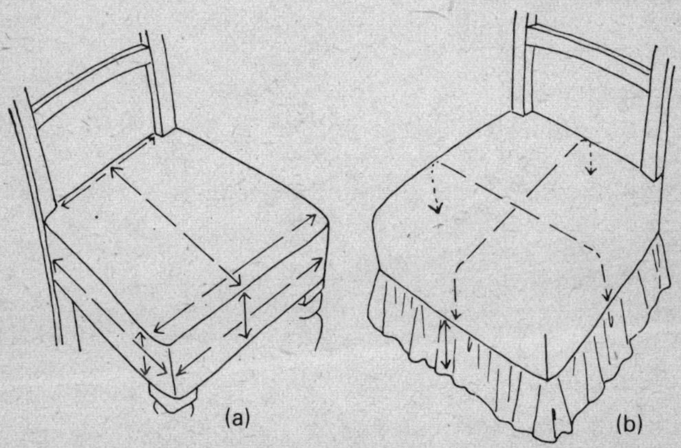

Figure 54   Chair covers (left) with piped border and tie-under, (right) with darts and gathered valance

Measuring
1.   *Chair*   (*a*)

	Initial measurements		After additions	
	across	down	across	down
(A) Seat top	46 cm	41 cm	48·5 cm	43·5 cm
	(18 in)	(16 in)	(19 in)	(17 in)
(B) Front border	46 cm	10 cm	48·5 cm	25 cm
	(18 in)	(4 in)	(19 in)	(10 in)
(C, D) Side borders (2)	39 cm	10 cm	41·5 cm	25 cm
	(15½ in)	(4 in)	(16½ in)	(10 in)
(E) Back border	30·5 cm	7·5 cm	33 cm	23 cm
	(12 in)	(3 in)	(13 in)	(9 in)

Additions
(*a*) Seam allowance to seat top, across and down   (2·5 cm – 1 in).
(*b*) Seam allowance to borders across   (2·5 cm – 1 in).
(*c*) Seam allowance and tie-under to borders down   (15 cm – 6 in).

2.   *Chair*   (*b*)

	Initial measurements		After additions	
	across	down	across	down
(A) Seat section	68 cm	60 cm	70·5 cm	62·5 cm
	(27 in)	(23½ in)	(28 in)	(24½ in)
Valance:				
(B) Front and Sides				
	130 cm	10 cm	200 cm	15 cm
	(51 in)	(4 in)	(79 in)	(6 in)
(C) Back	36·5 cm	10 cm	64 cm	15 cm
	(14½ in)	(4 in)	(25 in)	(6 in)

Note: On the cutting plan, the front and sides of the valance are cut in 4 pieces of 51 cm (20 in), using the remainder of the fabric after cutting the main piece (a). When joined, the strip will be approximately 200 cm (79 in) wide.

Additions
(*a*) Seam allowance to seat section across and down.
(*b*) Seam allowance and side hem to valance across plus fullness.
(*c*) Seam allowance and hem to valance down.

Cutting plan   (Fig. 55)

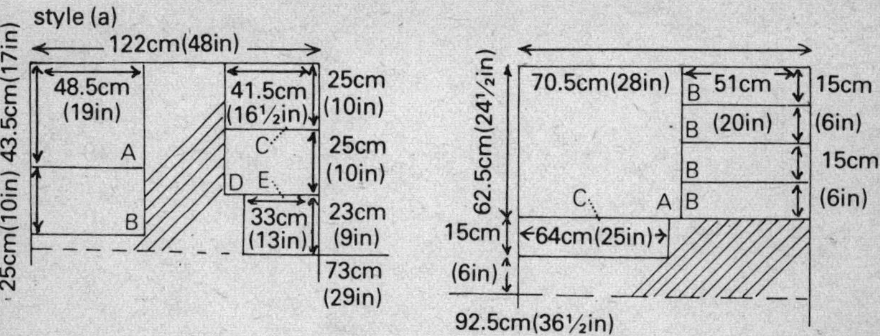

Figure 55   *Cutting plans for a chair cover*

Cutting out

Mark pieces in chalk on RS of the fabric before cutting out. Label each piece on WS near the *top* to indicate the correct way up when assembling. On a simple article like this chair it may not seem necessary, but on a large easy chair this is vital.

Fitting the cover   (Fig. 56)

1.   Very carefully mark the centre of the chair, dividing it in half down the middle with a line of pins (Fig. 56a).
2.   Fold each single section in half, RS out to show any pattern, and place the fold to the pin line, smoothing out to the edges. Ensure that the fold does not get pulled away from the centre.
3.   Where sections meet, pin the double raw edges together to fit snugly to the shape of the chair.
4.   Similarly, place sections cut twice WS together and pin in place on the chair, pinning seam lines to fit the shape (Fig. 56b or c).
5.   Where pieces have to fit round, for example, a back rail, make a diagonal slash in towards the wooden angle so that the fabric will lie flat (Fig. 56d (i), (ii) and (iii)).
6.   When sure of the correct fit, trim all pinned seams back to an even width (usually 13 mm ($\frac{1}{2}$ in)).
7.   Make *notches* in the raw edges at points that will help with assembly: (i) the centre fold; (ii) at the meeting points of seams; (iii) on either side of a dart or eased section.

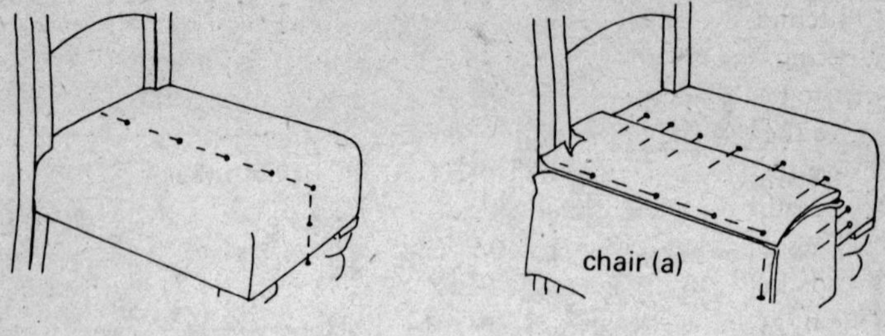

Figure 56a

Figure 56b

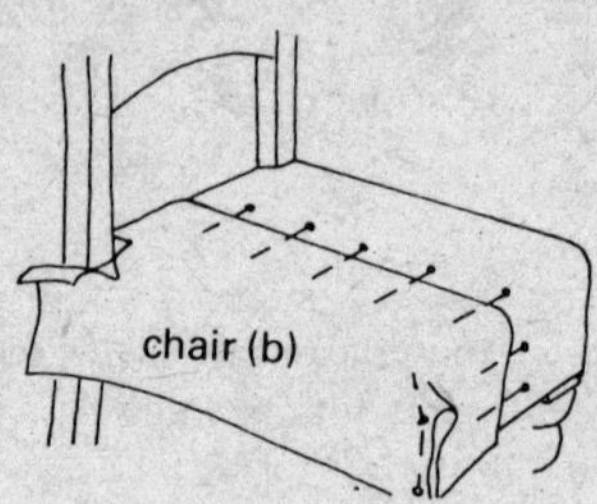

Figure 56c

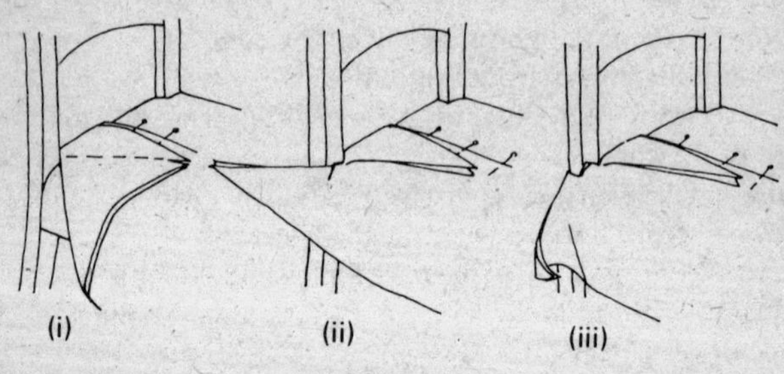

Figure 56d

8.   *Darts*   Where a lot of edge fullness needs to be removed, especially if matching two edges to form a seam, it is often neater to do this with darts (tapering tucks stitched on the WS) rather than with gathers. The darts need to be carefully fitted on the chair, making sure of the exact position where the dart tapers to nothing, and it is safer to thread-mark these to ensure they are even and match either side of the cover.

Threadmark with double thread, stabbing looped stitches through all thicknesses along the pinned line, and then remove the pins and cut the threads between the layers of fabric to leave small bits of thread in each section, giving a stitching line for the dart.

9.   *Tie-under*   For instructions on fitting and cutting this, *see* Chapter 6.

10.   *Valance*   Do not fit this until other cover sections have been made up. The position of the valance can then be chalked accurately on the fitted cover in relation to the floor level.

Assembling the cover

Carefully lift the fitted cover from the chair, disturbing the pins as little as possible and only removing them when ready to work that particular section.

1.   Prepare the piping, joining the casing and wrapping it round the cord.

2.   To stitch the darts, separate the double layers, clipping the thread-marks. Pin the darts along the marks and machine. Press small darts down. Large darts may be trimmed to seam width and pressed flat.

3.   Machine any seams that do not enclose the piping, e.g. joins at the border corners.

4.   Insert the piping in the seams that follow the style lines of the chair (e.g. round seat top of chair (a)).

5.   Neaten shaped sections that have been slashed to fit round the wood of the chair with a seam binding as for a tie-under (*see* Chapter 6).

For chair (a)

6.   Complete the tie-under as instructed in Chapter 6.

For chair (b)

6.   This chair will need a strap and facing fastening on either side at the back (*see* Chapter 6).

7.   Fit the cover on the chair and chalk-mark the position for the valance seam, measuring up from the floor level all round. Attach the prepared piping to this line.

8.   Make up the valance in two sections, one for the front and sides and one for the back. Mark the centre on both valance sections, and the corner positions on the section for the front and sides to ensure the even

distribution of the gathers. Allow for the back valance to extend round the corners with the strap of the fastening.

9.   Pin, tack and machine the valance to the cover, enclosing the piping.

On *both chair styles*, neaten the raw edges.
On Chair (b) hem strap and facing and attach hooks etc.

17 Bed covers

There are many styles of bed covers, but most of these are made applying
the same principles used in the articles already covered. A fitted divan cover
is made like a loose cover with a valance; a bed-base cover is simply a
valance set on to a bed-sized rectangle; a simple throw-over bedspread can
be made similarly to an un-headed curtain.

Pillow rise   (Fig. 57)
One problem peculiar to bedcovers is how to accommodate the pillow rise,
and this may be done in a number of ways, depending on the style of cover,
height of pillows, and whether the bed is single of double.

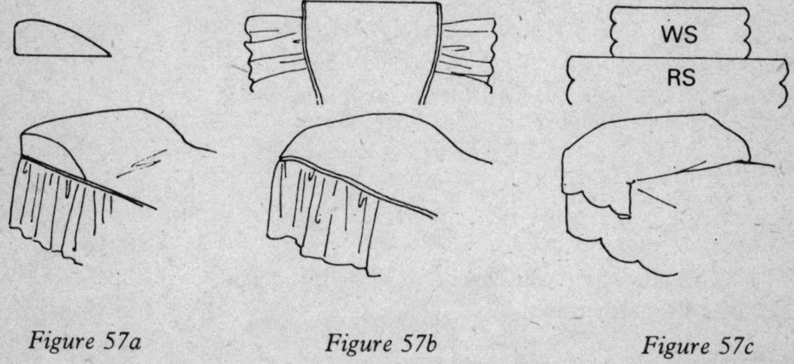

Figure 57a   Figure 57b   Figure 57c

1.   On throw-over spreads it is generally ignored except in so far as
allowing sufficient length to accommodate it.
2.   If a bolster or more than one pillow is used, the rise can be accommodated in a *pillow wedge* – a wedge-shaped border piece set in each side.
This is really only suitable for a double bed where the pillows come to the
edge of the mattress; if they don't the wedge is inclined to sag and look
untidy (Fig. 57a).

3.   On bedspreads with a plain platform and gathered or pleated sides, the pillow rise can be accommodated by gradually shaping out the pillow end of the platform. Take a measurement across the pillow rise and add the extra amount either side of the platform, starting shaping from where the pillow rise begins. This ensures a straight line running along the edge of the platform where it meets the valance (Fig. 57b).

4.   An attractive way of accommodating pillows is to add a flap to the end of the platform, set the reverse way round, that is taken under the pillows and drawn up from the back covering them and tucking down in front (Fig. 57c).

Measuring for bedcovers   (Fig. 58)

Measurements must always be taken over any bedding that would normally be on the bed beneath the cover.

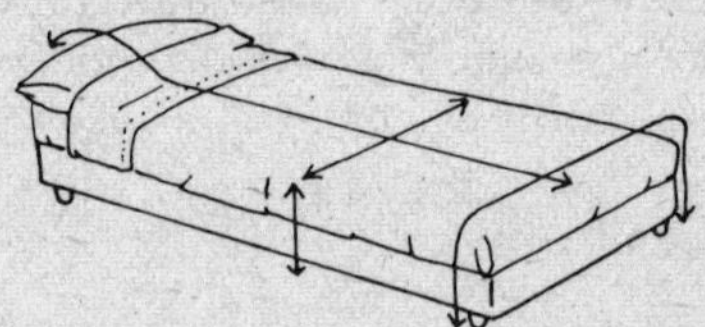

Figure 58   Measuring for a fitted bed cover

Length
The length is measured along the platform over the pillows from foot to head.

   Tuck-in allowance will depend on style but usually is about 30–45 cm (12 in–18 in) either end.

Width
The width is measured in three stages:

(*a*) from the floor to the platform;
(*b*) across the platform;
(*c*) right over the bed from floor to floor so that the tape curves over the edges of the bed but does not pull them down.

   The actual cover width can now be adjusted by adding twice measurement (*a*) to measurement (*b*) and comparing it with measurement (*c*) which is likely to be less because of rounding the corners.

   Subtract from the width measurement the distance you wish the spread to hang from the floor.

Measuring for bed-base cover
Measurements for this must be taken from the mattress over which it is to
hang, and it will be necessary to take a template of the corner shaping of
the mattress foot.

To make a throw-over bedspread   (Fig. 59)

This is the simplest kind to make but is fairly extravagant on fabric because
of the corner fullness.

To measure
Measure the bed as described bearing in mind the distance the spread is to
hang from the floor, which, if a divan, must be the same all round.

Allowance for hem
1.   For an *unlined* spread add 16 cm (6 in) to the width and length to
allow for a 4 cm (1½ in) double hem all round.
2.   For a *lined* spread add 8 cm (3 in) to the width and length to allow
for a 4 cm (1½ in) single hem all round.
Allowance for joins
It is usually necessary to join a 122 cm (48 in) fabric to give sufficient width
and as the width must be centred with additional strips either side, an
additional 5–8 cm (2 in–3 in) will be needed to provide for the two joins.

Cutting plan   (Fig. 59)
This is for a spread (for a single bed) 200 cm × 280 cm (79 in × 108 in).
   The cutting plan in Fig. 59 shows that 576 cm (222 in) of fabric are
needed for a lined spread (590 cm would be needed for an unlined one).

Note: The maximum width of spread that can be cut from two widths of
122 cm (48 in) fabric is 230 cm (90 in); anything wider would need to cut
into a third width.

To make
Unlined
Join the centre panel to the sides with either a rolled seam, a flat seam using
the selvedges, or a welt seam (*see* Chapter 3). These two seams can be made
a feature of the spread, decorated with braid, embroidery or contrasting
fabric inset.
   Press a 4 cm (1½ in) double hem all round, mitring the corners, and
slip-hem in place.

Lined
1.   Cut lining to the same dimension as the top fabric, making it 2·5 cm

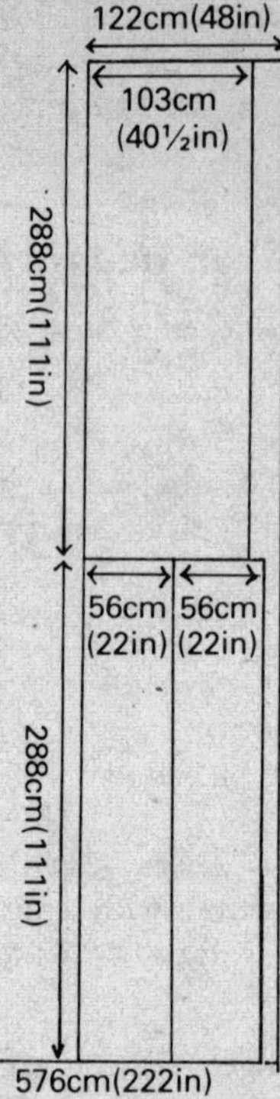

Figure 59a   *Cutting plan for a bedspread*

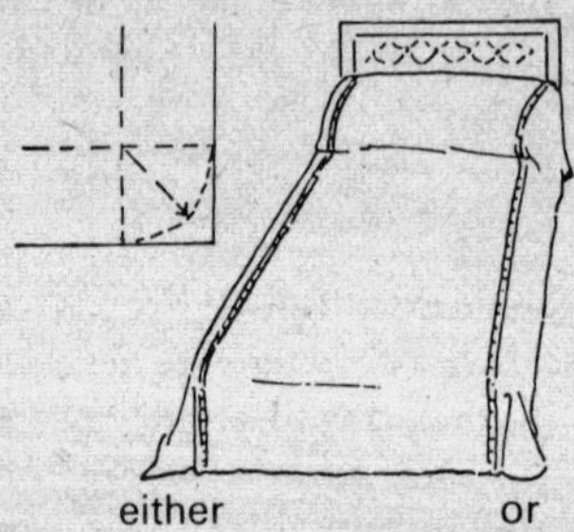

Figure 59b   *Bedspread corner treatments*

(1 in) smaller all round. Join the fabric and lining with flat seams either side of the central panel.

2.   On the fabric turn under and press a 4 cm (1½ in) single hem all round, mitring the corners. Serge-stitch in place.

3.   Set the lining to the fabric, matching seams, and then fold back and lock the lining to the fabric similarly to a lined curtain.

4.   Turn under the edges of the lining to give a 2·5 cm (1 in) margin and slip-stitch in place.

Corner treatment   (Fig. 59b)

Some people like the corners of a throwover spread rounded level with the sides, rather than hanging in points. This must be done before neatening the hem.

Mark the position of the platform foot on the spread (giving equal over-hang at sides and foot) and, taking the platform corner as a centre point, chalk in a curve with a radius equal to the depth of the overhang. Trim away surplus fabric to give an even hem depth all round.

To make a bed-base cover

Measurements needed

(*a*) Size of mattress top.
(*b*) Shape of corners (template).
(*c*) Depth of valance.

Estimating and cutting the valance is done exactly as described under '*valances*', calculating the fullness according to the type of gathers or pleats planned to go round the sides of the mattress, which could be each side only, round foot and sides, or all round on a divan without a headboard.

If the valance is not being taken across the head end of the mattress, the platform is formed at that end into a fitted flap which tucks round the mattress, helping to keep the bed base cover in position; an allowance for this is added to the platform measurement.

Facing strips   It is usual to set on facing strips, of the same fabric as the valance, round the edge of the platform to give the impression when set on the bed that the platform, which is made of cheap lining fabric, is of the same fabric as the valance.

Cutting plan   (Fig. 60)

This is for a bed-base cover with lined gathered valance round three sides of single bed.

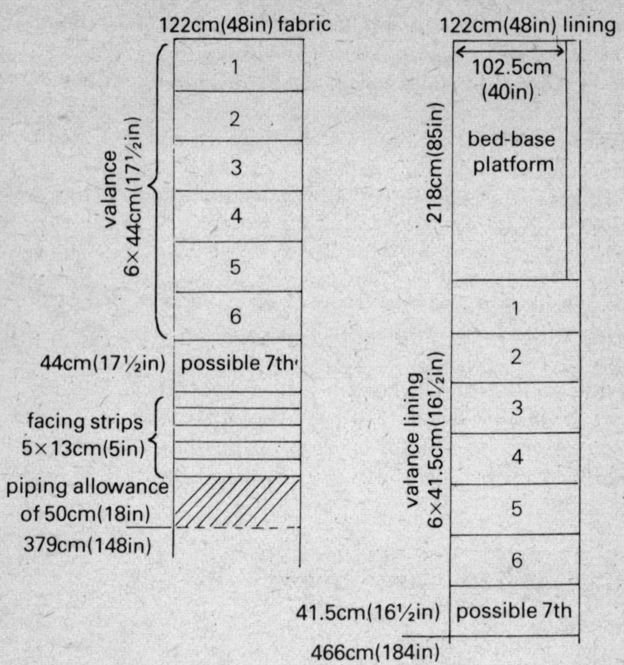

Figure 60   *Cutting plan for a bed-base cover*

Mattress size   – 100 cm × 200 cm
(3 ft 3 in × 6 ft 6 in)
Valance depth – 40 cm (16 in)

Allowances

Platform   – width 2·5 cm (1 in) for seams
length 18 cm (7 in) for seams
and flap

Valance   – width 1½ times fullness
depth 4 cm (1½ in) for seam
and hem (lining 2·5 cm (1 in) shorter)

Valance fullness   Bearing in mind that the width of the valance will be cut across 122 cm (48 in) wide fabric, 6 widths will give 732 cm (288 in) and 7 widths will give 854 cm (336 in) less about 20 cm (8 in) used in seam joins and side hems, whereas the calculated width is about 770 cm (300 in).

This is a case where you have to make your own mind up whether to cut 6 widths with slightly less gathers or 7 widths with more, and much will depend on the weight and drape of the fabric chosen.

Making up   (Fig. 61)
Platform
1.   Join up the facing strips and arrange RS up round three sides of the platform matching raw edges of platform to outer raw edge of strip. Form flat mitres at the corners. Tack in place along the platform edge (Fig. 61a).
2.   Turn under the inner raw edge of the strip and edge stitch to the platform.
3.   Shape platform corners to template, marking the shape with chalk and trimming away surplus to give seam allowance (Fig. 61b).

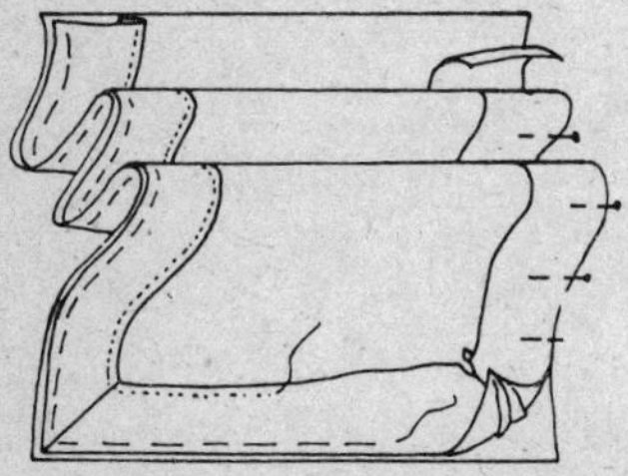

Figure 61a

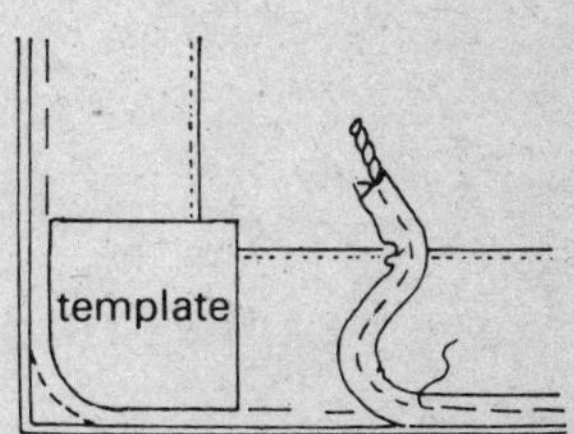

Figure 61b

4.   Prepare piping and attach it to the platform edge where the valance is to be stitched, leaving 16·5 cm (6½ in) free at the head end for the flap.
5.   Make up the *valance* as described under '*valances*'.
6.   Divide and mark the prepared valance into sections proportionate to the three sides of the platform (Fig. 61c).
7.   Divide up the platform similarly to ensure equal distribution of fullness (Fig. 61c).
8.   Gather up the top of the valance and set to the platform, matching the marks and enclosing the piping. Pin, tack and machine in position.
9.   Neaten raw edges.
10.   Form a double hem at the raw edge of the flap and fold it down on WS stitching it by hand to the sides of the valance.

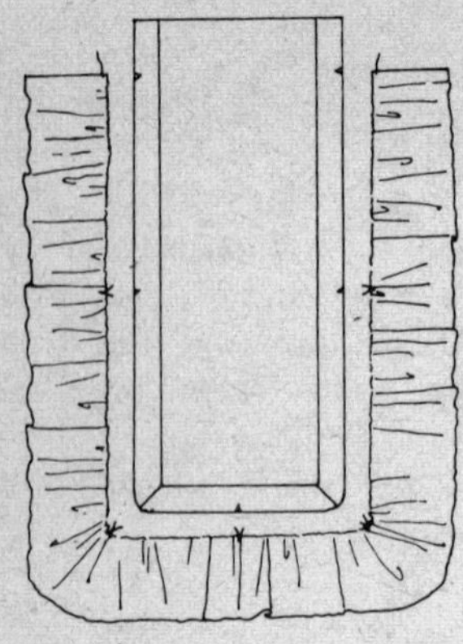

Figure 61c

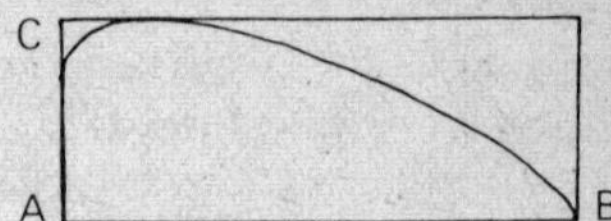

Figure 62   Making a pillow wedge on a fitted bedcover

More bedding information

To make a *pillow wedge* on a fitted bedcover:

1.   Measure the platform *length* in the usual way over the pillow rise and add about 30–50 cm (12–20 in) down behind the pillow to the base of the mattress. Platform *width* will be that of the mattress and bedding.

2.   Draft a wedge-shaped section as Fig. 62, A–B being the length of the side of the pillow (usually about 50 cm (19 in–20 in) plus turnings and A–C being height of pillow(s) (varying from 15 cm–25 cm (6 in–10 in)) plus turnings. Draw a gentle curve up from B to C and round off the corner at C.

3.   Set the wedge in between the platform and side border or frill. To ensure correct positioning, mark carefully the length A–B from the head end of the side border (of frill) before setting in the wedge to this position. The tuck-in allowed at the head end of the platform can be sewn to the end of the border or frill thus enclosing the mattress end.

Metrication

Introduction in some countries of metric sizing into the beds and bedding has caused some confusion, and a table of useful comparative measurements is set out on opposite page.

Sizing of beds and bedding

	Small single	Standard single	Small double	Standard double	King size
Imperial size	2 ft 6 in × 6 ft	3 ft × 6 ft 3 in	4 ft 6 in × 6 ft 3 in	5 ft × 6 ft 3 in	
Metric size	90 cm × 190 cm	100 cm × 200 cm	135 cm × 190 cm	150 cm × 200 cm	
Imperial sheet size	70 in × 104 in	70 in × 104 in	80 in × 104 in	90 in × 104 in	
Metric sheet size	175 cm × 255 cm 200 cm × 275 cm	175 cm × 275 cm 200 cm × 275 cm	230 cm × 255 cm 230 cm × 275 cm	230 cm × 275 cm	270 cm × 295 cm
Imperial Duvet	54 in × 78 in	54 in × 78 in	72 in × 78 in	78 in × 78 in	84 in × 78 in
Metric Duvet	137 cm × 198 cm	137 cm × 198 cm	183 cm × 198 cm	198 cm × 198 cm	
Yardage needed for Duvet cover	$4\frac{1}{2}$ yd of 70 in $3\frac{1}{8}$ yd of 90 in	$3\frac{1}{2}$ yd of 80 in $2\frac{1}{4}$ yd of 108 in	$4\frac{1}{8}$ yd of 80 in $4\frac{1}{8}$ yd of 90 in $4\frac{1}{8}$ yd of 108 in	$4\frac{5}{8}$ yd of 80 in $4\frac{5}{8}$ yd of 90 in $4\frac{5}{8}$ yd of 108 in	$4\frac{3}{4}$ yd of 80 in $4\frac{5}{8}$ yd of 90 in $4\frac{5}{8}$ yd of 108 in

Note: The metric pillow size will be 50 cm × 75 cm coming midway between the imperial sizes 19 in × 29 in and 20 in × 30 in.

Quilts

Continental quilt covers are very easy to make. The cover is simply a large bag formed by joining front and back together with a plain seam down the sides and top. The bottom edge is left open to insert the quilt pad and is usually neatened with a hem to which is attached a suitable fastening – ties, press studs or Velcro.

It is seldom cheaper to make the actual quilt pad. Both pad cover and filling are fairly expensive to buy, and the pad has to be made with channels (*see* Chapter 8) in order to keep the top and bottom of the quilt apart. As a rule from five to eight 2 cm ($\frac{3}{4}$ in) deep walls are stitched down the length of the quilt.

Traditional quilts

These were always stitched on a huge frame in the past. Making one this way without a frame is not easy as careful tacking at about 5–10 cm (2 in–4 in) intervals in both directions is needed to hold the fabric, padding and backing firmly in position.

It is possible to make small quilts on a domestic sewing machine although large ones are difficult to control because of the amount of bulk passing under the body of the machine; again without very careful tacking, and leaving pins in until the last moment, the fabric and backing will move and pucker. Choose a simple design – plain squares or diamonds are best – and not too thick padding (the Courtelle wadding 6 mm ($\frac{1}{4}$ in) thick is ideal – *see* Chapter 7).

When calculating measurements for a quilted article always allow for 'take-up' in the quilting which will reduce the finished size from that of the unquilted fabric by about 1 in 10, depending on the depth of filling and amount of stitching involved in the quilting design.

The stages in making a quilt are:

1. Cut fabric, wadding and lining to the required size and make any joins in each. Join wadding edges by lightly oversewing together without an overlap.

2. Mark out the quilting design on RS of top fabric. This can be done in chalk, hard pencil or, traditionally by 'needle marking' (pressing into the fabric with a blunt-pointed needle).

3. Divide the top and lining into quarters, giving an exact centre mark.

4. On a large flat surface place the lining WS up, cover with wadding, and smooth the top fabric over the wadding, design side uppermost matching raw edges, quarter marks and corners. Pin and tack round the edge.

5. Pin and tack the quarter lines through all thicknesses, checking an

exact match of lining and top fabric.

6.   Pin the quilting design through, checking for puckering. Turn the quilt over to the lining side and check the fabric is even between pinned sections, then again from RS tack all design lines through, leaving pins in. If these tacking lines do not provide sufficiently close tacking, add extra lines where required.

7.   Machine in design lines, removing pins as you stitch.

8.   Quilt edges can be finished in various ways:

(*a*) Turn the edges of the top and backing fabric under and slip stitch the two together.

(*b*) Apply a double bind, mitring corners (*see* Chapter 10).

(*c*) Trim back the wadding to leave about 2·5 cm (1 in) clear at edge, turn the lining and fabric edge together over to form a double hem and hem down, mitring corners.

Tie-quilting

A more simple way of containing the padding in a wadded quilt, particularly suited to patchwork, is tie-quilting. This involves knotting a strong thread through the layers at intervals of, say, 12–15 cm (5–6 in). In square patchwork, each corner of a square could be tied. A needle threaded with strong thread is stabbed down and back through the thicknesses and knotted firmly, the ends then being run back into the padding.

Adding a plain border to a quilted centre

Attractive bed covers involving less work can be made with only the platform quilted and a plain border or valance added round the sides. An economical way of adding a plain border is to cut mitred strips of fabric and lining, joining them in the form of a double mitre, to frame the quilt.

Method

For a single bed with platform 91 cm × 190 cm (3 ft × 6 ft 3 in) and valance depth of 40 cm (15½ in) (Fig. 63).

Cutting calculations

The quilted platform needs to be about 94 cm × 230 cm (37 in × 90½ in).

Additions to platform measurement being:

3 cm (1 in) to width for seams.

40 cm (15½ in) to length for seam at foot and tuck-in over pillow, plus the top hem allowance of 5 cm (2 in).

   Fig. 63a shows how the quilt is assembled and the finished size.

Size of cut border strips will be as follows:

Depth: 40 cm (15½ in) + 2·5 cm (1 in) hem + 15 mm (½ in) seam = 44 cm (17 in).

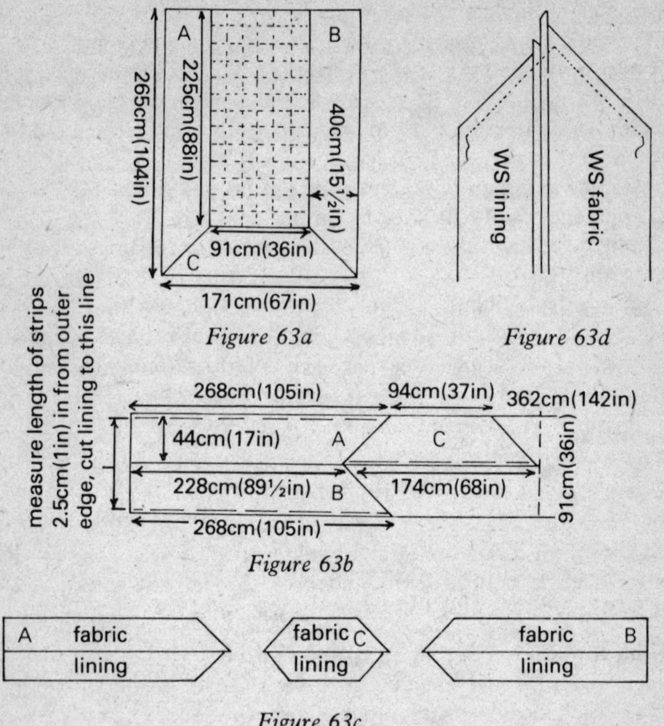

Figure 63a

Figure 63d

Figure 63b

Figure 63c

Length:

1. *Inner edge of strips* will be matched to the platform side to which they are to be sewn, plus turning allowance, i.e.:

Two side strips: 225 cm (88½ in) + 3 cm (1 in) = 228 cm (89½ in)

One foot strip: 91 cm (36 in) + 3 cm (1 in) = 94 cm (37 in)

2. *Outer edge of strips* will need to have added the amount of the border depth. In the case of the side strips, this will only be added to one side (at the foot); in the case of the strip along the foot, the addition must be on either side, i.e.:

Two side strips: 228 cm (89½ in) + 40 cm (15½ in) = 268 cm (71 in)

One foot strip: 94 cm (37 in) + 80 cm (31 in) = 174 cm (68 in)

Cut the border strips as *cutting plan* (Fig. 63b).

Cut the *lining* the same as the fabric less 2·5 cm (1 in) at the lower edge marked on cutting plan).

To make
1.   Take each fabric strip and join to its corresponding lining strip along the lower (longest) edge, matching raw edges, so that borders A, B and C look as Fig. 63c.
2.   Pin the mitred edges together, A to C and B to C, RS together, and machine along the seam line so that the point of the mitre comes, not at the join between the lining and fabric, but 13 mm ($\frac{1}{2}$ in) within the fabric side (Fig. 63d) and centrally between the outer raw edges. Press the seam flat and trim away surplus at the point to reduce bulk.
3.   Fold both unmitred ends of the border WS out, matching raw edges so that the seam between the lining and fabric comes 13 mm ($\frac{1}{2}$ in) up from the lower folded edge. Seam up the ends and turn through to the RS. Check the border for accuracy of fit to quilted centre platform and press.
4.   Tack the top raw edges of the lining and fabric together all round.
5.   Fold back the lining of the quilted platform out of the way and match the quilted edge to the border, RS facing, taking care to match the corners. The head end of the platform will extend for the depth of the hem allowance, beyond the border pieces A and B. Machine the top and wadding to the border all round.
6.   Turn under the raw edge of the platform lining and hem down over machining, enclosing raw edges. Neaten head end of platform with a small hem, or turn in edges and slip-stitch.

Eiderdowns

The need here is usually to repair an existing one either by replacing the whole cover or recovering one side.

1.   Replacing cover
The cover must be of down-proof cambric, which is available in various colours and patterns. Alternatively a lightweight fabric may be mounted on to down-proof cambric but this does increase the weight and is usually done on one side only, the underside being kept to plain down-proof cambric.

Measuring must be done carefully along the outer edge and a new 'bag' cut allowing 15 mm ($\frac{5}{8}$ in) for turnings. A double eiderdown will need an additional border beyond the fabric width with flat mitres at each corner. Mark out the quilting pattern on the top cover (RS) with tacking thread, then join the top and bottom sections together enclosing the piping or frill if required (and leaving an opening for the filling. Turn the bag through to the RS and carefully pin through the marked design to the underneath of the eiderdown. Machine the design, leaving openings for working in the filling. Fill the new bag from the old eiderdown by sewing openings together and patting the down through, having previously unpicked the machine stitching of the design on the old eiderdown. Sew up the opening and complete stitching of the design.

2.   *To cover just one side of an old eiderdown*, cut off the old piping or frill. Carefully measure the size and quilting design. Cut a new top cover with a 15 mm (⅝ in) turning allowance and mark out the design on the RS. Attach the piping or frill round the outer edge of the new cover, then turn the raw edge under and slip-stitch to the old eiderdown all round the edge to hide the removal of old piping. Pin down the design, checking for puckering. Tack and machine design.

18 Handling canvas-work

Canvas work (often erroneously called 'tapestry') is becoming increasingly popular, and people often want to make it into cushions. This is not difficult as long as certain rules are observed.

1. Try to ensure, if canvas work is intended to be rectangular, that all corners are as nearly as possible right-angles. If the embroidery is badly distorted it can be stretched professionally, or, if a board slightly larger than the canvas is available, it is possible to do the stretching yourself by placing some clean damp blotting paper or cloth beneath the work, then pinning the canvas into shape and letting it dry naturally. (Keep the pins well away from the embroidery in case of rust marks.)
2. It is easier for a beginner to make the cushion up neatly if piping is omitted. A cord added after can look just as attractive.
3. It is also easier to sew up the opening rather than insert a fastener because of the stiffness and bulk of the canvas.

Making-up   (without piping)
1. Work from the canvas side and, using matching thread, tack the canvas to the fabric back all round following a canvas thread immediately beside the embroidery stitching. Take smaller tacking stitches than usual and work a backstitch between every two or three tacking stitches. These tacking stitches will be left in the work.
2. Using a piping foot, machine carefully round, again stitching immediately alongside the embroidery, leaving an opening for the pad to be inserted.
3. Turn the cushion through (unpicking tacking across opening) and check that no canvas is visible round the seam. If it is, restitch that section.
4. Trim canvas back to about a 15 mm ($\frac{5}{8}$ in) seam allowance, clip away some corner bulk, and immediately neaten the raw edges, starting with a single edge along the opening.
5. Insert the pad and sew up the opening, again following canvas thread, close to the embroidery.

To make up with piping
1.   Prepare piping, setting the cord into the casing, and with matching thread tack firmly round the edge of the canvaswork, working from the WS of the canvas and feeling the position of the cord with the fingers to ensure that it comes close to the stitching line. Clip casing to turn the corners neatly.
2.   Machine piping along the position of the opening only.
3.   Apply the back section of the cushion to the canvaswork following the previous instructions for an unpiped cushion.

A small canvas embroidery can be used for a cushion if it is 'framed' by a fabric border to enlarge it to a suitable size with strips mitred at the corners.

To 'frame' an embroidery with a fabric border (Fig. 64)

Planning
This is the most important part of the project as the actual making up only involves working four flat mitres.

Accurately *measure* the size of the worked canvas, e.g. a rectangle 20 cm × 25 cm (8 in × 10 in). If an equal width border with 45° mitres is planned this will enlarge it in the same proportions as the design but, of course, it is also possible to make the finished cushion square by adding side strips wider or narrow than the top and bottom with mitres at a different angle.

Cutting plan   (Fig. 64a)
To make a cushion front 30 cm × 35 cm (12 in × 14 in) from an embroidery 20 cm × 25 cm (8 in × 10 in) (Fig. 64).

Border
Depth: 5 cm (2 in) + seams (2) of 15 mm ($\frac{1}{2}$ in) = 8 cm (3 in).
Inner length: To match sides of canvas work plus seam allowance (15 mm ($\frac{1}{2}$ in) = 23 cm (9 in) and 28 cm (11 in)).
Outer length: As above plus depth of border each side = 33 cm (13 in) and 38 cm (15 in).

Note: As the strips slope at each end and take in a seam allowance it is difficult to calculate the exact length to cut each outer and inner edge. The safest way is to allow extra at the outer edges beyond the measured seam allowance, then chalk in the finished size of the strips on the fabric and cut them with a seam allowance all round.

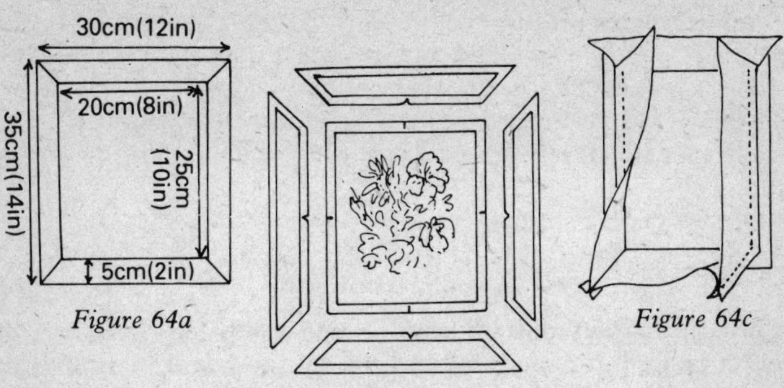

Figure 64a

Figure 64c

Figure 64b

To make up

1.   Mark the centre down each side of the canvas embroidery and the corresponding centre on each strip (Fig. 64b).

2.   With RS together, matching the centre marks, and following the line of canvas thread next to embroidery, tack the inner seam line of each border strip in place, stopping exactly at corner of embroidery. Machine along tacking line.

3.   In turn, bring the RS of each corner mitre together and tack along chalked mitre line. Check that it lies flat and that the proportion of the rectangle is accurate, and adjust if necessary (Fig. 64c).

4.   Machine mitres carefully by inserting the needle exactly where the previous stitching line stopped and machine out to the corner of the cushion. Press the seam flat.

5.   Trim the seams back to the regular seam allowance and neaten. You will find that the seam joining embroidery to the border will want to lie so that the canvas is flat and the seam allowance of the border turns back, producing a framed effect.

6.   Complete the cushion in the usual way.

Materials and suppliers

The majority of soft furnishing needs are available at good stores and soft furnishings specialist shops everywhere, but in case of difficulty, the following information may help.

Branches of the John Lewis Partnership in the UK, besides selling most haberdashery items, stock the following items mentioned in this book: Circular needles, piping cord, Velcro, Milium lining, bump lining, narrow buckram both for curtains and for pelmets, filled cushion pads, 'Spantape' and Rufflette heading tapes, do-it-yourself blind kits. (Besides London branches, there are stores in Newcastle-upon-Tyne, Windsor, Sheffield, Reading, Nottingham, Portsmouth, Liverpool, Edinburgh, Cambridge, Watford, Southampton and Milton Keynes.)

Velcro, the touch and close fastener
In case of difficulty contact:
UK: Selectus Ltd, Biddulph, Stoke-on-Trent, TS8 7RH.
USA: Velcro International Ltd, 681 Fifth Avenue, NY10022.
Australia: Velcro Australia (Pty) Ltd, 31 Queen Street, Melbourne 3000.
South Africa: Velcro Africa (Pty) Ltd, c/o E. I. Rogoff Ltd, PO Box 7296, Johannesburg.

Milium
This lining is unfortunately only available through outlets in the UK. Enquiries to: Milium Promotion Centre, St Ann's House, St Ann's Place, Manchester, M2 7LP.

Various specialist interlinings
These can be purchased from MacCulloch and Wallis Ltd, 25/26 Dering Street, London, W1R 0BH who also stock a wide range of haberdashery items.

Decorative headings for curtains
Spantape Services Ltd, Mersey Industrial Estate, Heaton Mersey, Stockport, SK4 3EQ market speciality curtain tapes which draw up into various

decorative shirred effects – 'Smocked', 'Tudor Ruff', and 'Trellis', as well as the conventional pleats. Available at good stores, including JLP.

Curtain fittings and headings
Swish Products Limited cover retail outlets all over the UK, Australia and South Africa manufacturing a wide range of suspension systems (Tamworth, Staffs., B79 7TW).

Rufflette Limited market tracks, heading tapes, hooks, cord tidies etc., including detachable lining tape; also 'Matchups' range of decorative trimmings (Sharston Road, Manchester, M22 4TH).

Fillings

Foam
Dunlopreme Foam is available worldwide and can be bought at most upholstery and do-it-yourself shops. Specialist advice in UK can be obtained from Dunlop Semtex Ltd, Chester Road, Erdington, Birmingham, B35 7AL, and information on availability from Retail Sales Dept, Dunlopillo, Pannal, Harrogate, North Yorks., HG3 1JL, or from the factory in the relevant country.

Cushion fillings
Beckfoot Mill, (specialists in washable fillings), Beckfoot Lane, Harden, Bingley, BD16 1AR.

Polystyrene granules
Available through mail order from Arrowtip Ltd, Arrowtip House, 31–35 Stannary Street, Kennington, London, SE11.

General haberdashery, Fillings etc.
Russell Trading Co., 75 Paradise Street, Liverpool, L1 3 BP, sells a wide variety of soft furnishing items including fillings, linterfelt (thick upholstery wadding), down, feathers, down- and feather-proof fabrics etc.

Suggestions for further reading

Fabrics

The Butterick Fabric Handbook Edited by Irene Cumming Kleenberg (Butterick Publishing, 1975)
Fibres and Fabrics of Today by Helen Thomson (Heinemann, 1969)
Washing Wisdom by K. J. Mills (Forbes Pub. Ltd., 1970)
Technology of Textile Properties by Marjorie A. Taylor (Forbes Pub. Ltd., 1974)

Embroidery

Teach Yourself Embroidery by Lynette de Denne, 1977.
Encyclopaedia of Needlework by Th. de Dillmont (DMC Library, 1971) (This book is marvellous for different cords, fringes and other trims suitable for soft furnishings.)

Two good stitch books:
100 Embroidery Stitches (a J. and P. Coats 1967 publication which is consequently being reprinted)
Embroidery Stitches by Barbara Snook (Batsford, 1968)

Colour and design

Making the most of colour in the Home, by Alan Taylor (Published by ARCO Publications in 1968 but still available from public libraries).

More soft furnishing information

Soft Furnishing in the Home by Winifred Mitchell (Batsford, 1970)

Index